BRIDGE

PATRICK JOURDAIN

BLANDFORD

First published in Great Britain in 1990.
This new revised edition published in 1993 by
Blandford, Villiers House, 41–47 Strand, London
WC2N 5JE.

Designed by Anita Ruddell

Illustrations by Peter Bull

Photoset in 10/11pt Compugraphic Triumvirate
by BP Integraphics, Bath, Avon
Printed and bound in Great Britain by
Richard Clay Ltd, Bungay, Suffolk

0 7137 2408 0

Acknowledgements

The Author and Publishers would like to
thank Pergamon Press, Express
Newspapers (Frontispiece and p.67), The
English Bridge Union and Patrick Jourdain
for supplying photographs.

**Frontispiece: Omar Sharif, film actor,
and probably the world's best known
bridge player, seeks inspiration during
a tournament.**

CONTENTS

Foreword *6*

History & development of bridge 8

Equipment & Terminology 10

The game – a guide 16

Rules clinic 48

Technique
  of bidding 54
  of play 64

Useful addresses 77

Rules index 78

General index 79

FOREWORD

World-wide there are millions of people who play bridge; this is a game that we can take up young and play into our latter years – players in their nineties are not uncommon, and nowadays we even go on playing after we have notched up a century! So this is a game with a real future to it, for everyone!

Well done, then, to Ward Lock who have recognized the growing importance of Bridge and have accorded it a place in their popular 'Play the Game' series. I am sure they have hit on a winner, and many people will be drawn to a new leisure pursuit, which can be played both socially and competitively. The British Bridge League or any of the four Home Unions (England, Scotland, Wales, N. Ireland) will be pleased to put you in touch with clubs in your locality where you will find a welcome and make new friends.

And particularly well done to choose Patrick Jourdain as the author for the book. He is a knowledgeable bridge writer and teacher, up-to-date in his ideas, as well as being a fine player. He is the Principal of the Cardiff School of Bridge, and his experience there has taught him how to explain the game clearly to beginners; to the person who glances casually at this page I say simply that with Patrick you are in good hands.

So here is your starting point – come join the bridging throng, and may you enjoy many happy hours with the game and its people.

GRATTAN ENDICOTT
President of the British Bridge League

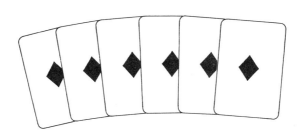

Pat Davies of Bristol ponders her next play. Miss Davies was a member of the British women's team that won the world title in 1981 and 1985.

HISTORY & DEVELOPMENT OF BRIDGE

Bridge is a card game for four people sitting round a table, where the players facing each other are partners. It is principally a game of deduction. Bridge and chess could be called the world's most popular mind-sports.

Bridge derived from whist at the end of the 19th century. It was most probably of Turkish or Russian origin, and was played by army officers in Egypt and India. Early in the 1890s the game arrived in both New York and London. The Portland Club in London took up the game in 1894 at the prompting of Lord Brougham who had learned it in India.

Bridge was distinguished from whist by the idea that the players could name the trump suit, and, during the play, by the exposure of one hand as 'dummy'. In 1904 the idea of naming trumps was extended into an auction where the players also stated how many tricks they would take during the play. In 1909 the Portland Club produced the first Laws of Auction Bridge and the game soon replaced whist in popularity.

In 1914 an idea from the French game, Plafond, was introduced to bridge in America. The scoring rewarded claims made during the bidding to make extra tricks in the play, provided, of course, the 'contract' was fulfilled. In 1925, during a Caribbean cruise aboard the *SS Finland*, Harold S Vanderbilt devised the scoring which led to Contract Bridge superseding Auction Bridge in popularity. The 'birthday' of modern bridge is popularly thought of as 1st November, 1925.

Laws of Contract Bridge, the game described in this book, were developed in New York in 1926 and in London, by the Portland Club, in 1929. By co-operation between bridge clubs in Britain, France, and the US, the first international laws were published in 1932. Further revisions have been made in 1935, 1963 and 1981. The Portland Club has retained an interest in all these revisions.

Most of the credit for the early rapid rise in the popularity of bridge is given to the Russian-born American, Ely Culbertson. In 1929 he founded the first contract bridge magazine (The Bridge World) and his celebrated 'Blue Book' was published in 1930.

Although bridge is a game of skill, the luck of the deal plays an important role.

Bridge as a competitive game received a substantial boost by the introduction of an idea used in whist tournaments in the 19th century. A deal was 'duplicated' at more than one table, and players subsequently compared their score with players at another table who had held identical cards. The principle of 'Duplicate' bridge eliminates much of the luck of the deal inherent in 'Rubber' bridge, the form of the game used when deals are not duplicated. There are minor differences in scoring between the two forms but both are contract bridge.

The American Contract Bridge League was formed in 1937 following the amalgamation of three competing bodies and took responsibility for organizing tournament bridge in the USA. The British Bridge League, which undertakes a similar role in Britain, was formed in 1938 from the separate Bridge Unions of England, Scotland, Wales and Northern Ireland.

In 1930 Culbertson organized a much publicised challenge match with a British team led by Colonel Walter Buller. The Americans won but the match was front page news in Britain and there was a rapid growth in the number of players.

The International Bridge League was formed in 1932 and six nations competed in Scheveningen. This first European Championship was won by Austria. The first official World Championship was held in 1935 between the champions of Europe (France), and the United States. The USA won but, two years later, Austria beat the USA in Budapest. (Austria also won the first women's world title held at the same time.) War then intervened and the world championships were not resumed until 1950 in Bermuda. The Bermuda Bowl has been played for regularly since.

In 1989, in Perth, Australia, Brazil became the first nation outside North America or Europe to win the Bermuda Bowl. Britain won the title in 1955, and won the women's title, for the Venice Cup,

in 1981 and 1985. A world championship for Juniors (under the age of 25) was launched in 1987 and won by Britain in 1989. These championships are organized by the World Bridge Federation which was formed in 1958.

The WBF organized the first World Bridge Olympiad in 1960 where 29 nations entered teams. France won the Open event, and the United Arab Republic won the women's contest of 14 nations. At the Olympiad held in Venice in 1988, over sixty nations fielded teams. The WBF also runs an annual event in which, on the same day all over the world, players compete (at their local heat) over the same set of deals. In 1989 over 80,000 bridge players entered this one event, earning an entry in the Guinness Book of Records. Each contestant received a booklet of the deals, compered by film actor and bridge player, Omar Sharif.

The World Bridge Federation now has over eighty member nations and estimates that the world has more than 90 million bridge-players. The Soviet Union is the most significant recent addition to the world bridge community. For many years chess was the only mind-sport which received official blessing within the USSR. In 1989, for the first time, an official Soviet team played in the European bridge championships. The 1991 World Championships, held in Killarney were won by Britain.

In Britain, more adults play bridge than soccer. The game suits an age range from 10 to 100. It costs no more than the price of a pack of cards to play. Enjoy your game!

EQUIPMENT & TERMINOLOGY

Bridge is an exceptionally cheap game to play. Once you have four players, all you need is a standard pack of playing cards and pencil and paper to keep score. It is helpful, though not essential, to have a suitable bridge table (a standard table is 2'6" square with green baize cover), four chairs and good light. Bridge scorepads, which look something like this:

can be acquired from a stationers but ordinary paper will do.

You are not likely to play duplicate bridge until you are more experienced and the equipment should be available at your local club. Duplicate bridge requires several packs of cards, the set of wallets (or 'boards') in which the cards for each of the four players are kept separately, and special stationery for scoring.

We	They

The standard bridge scorepad.

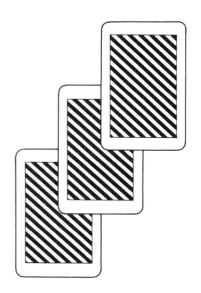

The cards

Just in case you are not familiar with a standard pack of 52 playing cards (no jokers are needed for bridge), we specify that the pack is divided into four suits: clubs(♣), diamonds(♦), hearts(♥), and spades(♠), and that each suit has 13 cards. These, in ascending order of rank, (in bridge, the ace counts high), are the 2 to the 10 in numerical order, followed by the picture (or court) cards jack (J), queen (Q) king (K), and finally, the ace (A).

The cards 10 up to the ace are called honour cards.

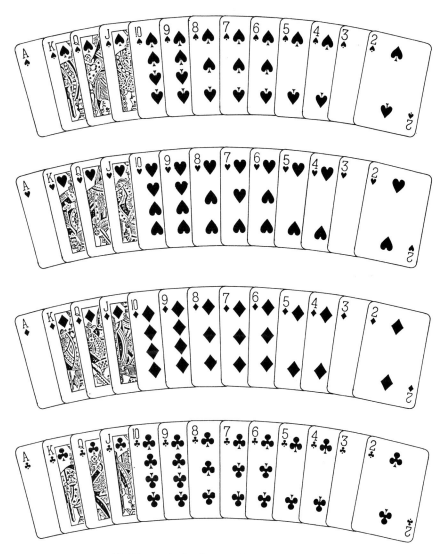

All 52 cards in the pack are used in bridge, 13 dealt to each of four players.

In bridge the suits themselves have a ranking which is relevant in selecting partners by cut, in the bidding and in scoring. Ascending order happens to be alphabetic order, i.e. clubs, diamonds, hearts, spades. During the play of the cards for a particular deal, one suit may have been named as trumps. The trump suit has added value in the play, otherwise all suits are of equal importance.

BRIDGE · TERMINOLOGY

Bridge terminology may not be meaningful to a novice but, for reference, it is best defined in alphabetical order. We therefore suggest you skip the next section for the moment, returning when you need to look up the definition of a word.

At the beginning of a game, the person to the dealer's left shuffles the cards and passes them to the person on the dealer's right to be cut. It may seem complicated at first, but it is a very fair and efficient way of getting on with play.

Auction The process of determining the contract by means of successive calls.

Bid An undertaking to win at least a specified number of odd tricks in a specified denomination.

Call Any bid, double, redouble, or pass made during the auction.

Contract The final bid in the auction becomes the contract for that deal. The bid may be undoubled, doubled or redoubled.

Convention Any call (or play) that, by prior agreement between partners, serves to convey a special meaning that the opponents cannot reasonably be expected to understand without an explanation.

Cut Either: the drawing of cards to determine partners **or:** the splitting of the pack prior to a deal, by the player on dealer's right.

2 cut

3 deal

1 shuffle

EQUIPMENT · & · TERMINOLOGY

Deal Either: the act of distributing the cards to the four players, **or:** the cards so distributed described as a unit, including the auction and play.

Declarer The player who, for the side that makes the final bid, first bid the denomination named in that bid.

Defender A member of the side opposing declarer.

Denomination The suit or notrump specified in a bid.

Discard Play of a card of a suit (not a trump), when void of the suit led to the trick.

Double A call over an opponent's bid, increasing the value of fulfilled contracts, and the penalty for defeated contracts.

Doubleton A suit holding in one hand of two cards.

Dummy Either: the partner of declarer, **or:** more properly, the cards held by declarer's partner which are spread face upwards on the table after the opening lead.

Entry A card that, by winning a trick, gives the next lead to the hand in which the card resided.

Finesse An attempt to win a trick with a card that is not the highest card out, in the hope that the opponent who played earlier to the trick held the higher card.

Follow Suit Play a card of the same suit as the card led to a trick.

Forcing A bid is forcing if, by agreement, the bidder's partner is not expected to allow it to become the final contract.

Game A unit in scoring achieved when one side has accumulated 100 or more trick points in contracts bid and made.

Hand The cards originally dealt to one player. Sometimes used to refer to a full deal.

Honour Any Ace, King, Queen, Jack or ten.

Laws The international rules of the game. Revisions for Rubber Bridge were published in 1981 and for Duplicate Bridge in 1987.

Lead The first card played to a trick.

Major Hearts and spades are the major suits.

Minor Clubs and diamonds are the minor suits.

Notrumps The denomination in which there is no trump suit.

No Bid See 'PASS'

Odd Trick Each trick won by declarer's side in excess of six.

Opening Lead The card led to the first trick.

Overcall A bid made after an opponent has made the first bid in an auction.

Overtrick Each trick won by declarer's side in excess of the contract.

Partner The player with whom one plays as a side against the other two players.

Partscore 90 or fewer trick points for contract(s) bid and made.

Pass A call specifying that the player does not at that turn elect to bid, double or redouble.

Penalty Either: the score for a defeated contract, counting against declarer's side or: the adjustment specified for a violation of the Laws.

Play The phase of the game in which cards are contributed from one's hand to a trick.

Point Count An assessment of the value of a hand by any numerical method.

Pre-Empt An unnecessarily high bid made with the intention of making it difficult for the opponents to bid.

Redeal A second or subsequent deal replacing a faulty deal.

Re-Bid A player's second or subsequent bid.

Redouble A call over an opponent's double increasing further the scoring value of fulfilled or defeated contracts.

Response A bid made by a player after partner has made the first bid for the side.

Revoke The play of a card of another suit by a player who is able to follow suit.

Rotation The order in which the right to deal, to call, or to play, progresses round the table to the left.

Rubber The scoring period that ends when one side has scored two games.

Ruff Play a trump when unable to follow suit to the card led to a trick.

Shuffle The mixing of the pack of cards prior to the deal.

Side The players who constitute a partnership against the other two players.

Side Suit In a trump contract, any suit other than trumps.

Singleton A suit holding in one hand of one card.

Slam A contract to win either twelve tricks (the Small Slam) or thirteen tricks (the Grand Slam).

Trick The unit by which the outcome of the contract is determined, regularly consisting of four cards, one contributed by each player in rotation beginning with the lead.

Trump Each card of the suit, if any, named in the contract.

Undertrick Each trick by which declarer's side falls short of fulfilling a contract.

Void A suit in which a hand has no cards.

Vulnerable A side that has won one game in a rubber is vulnerable. The scoring penalties for failing to fulfil a contract are increased, but higher premiums can be earned if the contract succeeds. A side that has not won a game in a rubber is non-vulnerable.

Roland Rohowsky was a member of the German team which won the World Bridge Olympiad held in Geneva in 1990. Rohowsky, at the age of 22 became the youngest world bridge champion.

THE GAME –
A GUIDE

Bridge is a partnership game. The four players sit round the table and we shall refer to their position by the points of the compass, thus:

The players sitting opposite each other are partners, the other two are their opponents. North-South are playing against East-West. Any plus score

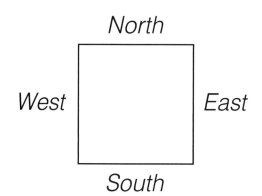

Throughout this book, the four players around the table are called 'North', 'South', 'East' and 'West', to remind you who is playing what, and where they are sitting. North and South are a team, trying to beat the partnership of East and West.

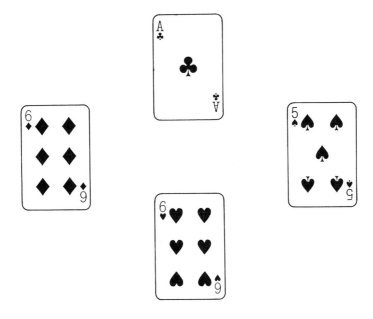

To choose the partners, each player picks a card, and those with the two highest cards make one partnership, the two lowest are the opposition. If two players pick cards with the same face value, as here, then spades is higher than hearts, hearts is higher than diamonds, and diamonds is higher than clubs. Of course when you are starting to play bridge for the first time, you can choose your own partners.

achieved by one side is a minus score for the opponents. What is good for North must also be good for South but bad for East and West.

We now describe exactly what happens when four players start a game of bridge and you can use the guide as a script, following the actions precisely. But first, if you do not know any of the other three players, please introduce yourselves!

Choice of Partners

The choice of partners is usually decided by a draw. A shuffled pack of cards (no jokers) is spread face downwards on the table and the players draw one card each. The players who draw the two highest cards will partner each other. The seniority in the rank of the cards, starting with the highest, is ace, king, queen jack, followed by the 'spot' cards, 10 down to 2: i.e.

A K Q J 10 9 8 7 6 5 4 3 2

If two players draw a card of the same

rank, then the seniority of the suit is used to determine which is higher. The seniority of the suits is important elsewhere in the game, so remember it carefully. It is in alphabetic order starting with the lowest, i.e. clubs(♣), diamonds(♦), hearts(♥), spades(♠).

Example: the four players draw the five of spades, the six of hearts, the six of diamonds, and the ace of clubs. Who are partners?

Answer: the highest card is the ace, the lowest is the five; as the six of hearts is senior to the six of diamonds the six of hearts partners the ace, and the six of diamonds partners the five.

The player who draws the highest card is given choice of seat. (To save time, we will use 'he' and 'him' throughout this book, but remember that the numbers of men and women playing bridge are approximately the same). His partner must sit opposite and the other two fill in as they please.

The deal

The ritual of the deal follows. This ritual was developed in the days of whist more than a century ago with two objectives in mind. The use of three players reduced the chance of manipulating the deck, and the whole procedure is efficient in the use of time. It is usual, though not essential, to have two packs of cards of different colour in use. One pack can be shuffled ready for a later deal while the other is being dealt for the current one (you see how bridge-players hate to waste a moment in the preliminaries).

The player who drew the highest card, (who is going to deal first), selects one pack of cards to be shuffled by the opponent on his left. The pack is then passed across the table to the shuffler's partner (the player to dealer's right), who cuts the pack by taking off a top portion of the deck and placing it nearer to the dealer. The dealer lifts the bottom portion which is further from him, places it on top of the deck and begins to deal one card at a time in clockwise rotation round the table, starting with the player on his left and continuing until he has run out of cards. If all goes well the dealer's last card should go to himself. Meanwhile, if there were two packs of cards, the dealer's partner has been shuffling the other pack of cards in preparation for the next deal. As the duty of dealing goes round the table to the left, the shuffler of this second deck places the deck by the player on his right. There is a harsh little ditty to remind the shuffler of this: 'If of sense you are bereft, place the cards upon your left; if you're not demented quite, place the cards upon your right'.

All that sounds complicated, and the game has not even started! But if you follow the instructions with four players sitting at the table you soon acquire the knack, and the deal can be disposed of in a matter of seconds.

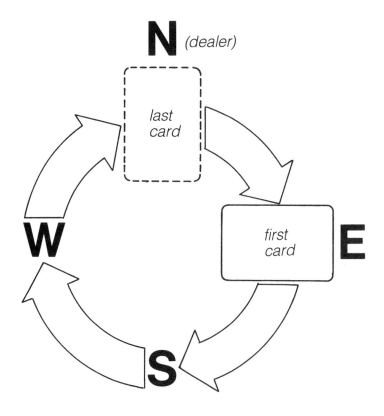

Always deal in a clockwise direction, beginning with the player on your left. The last card should be yours.

Sorting your Cards

When the deal is complete, each player should have a pile of 13 cards face downwards in front of him. It is considered proper to wait until all the cards are dealt before looking at any you receive. You are advised to count your cards face downwards to check you have 13 before looking at them. In this way a mis-deal is discovered before the players know whether they have a good or bad hand. If all is well, pick up your cards, and, concealing them from the view of the other three players, have a look. We suggest you sort them into suits, and into ascending sequence within the suits. However, we do not recommend putting the suits in the seniority ranking (clubs, diamonds, hearts, spades) because that puts the two red suits next to each other, which can lead to confusing the suits.

Better is to alternate the colours, putting a red suit next to a black. Your hand may then look like this:

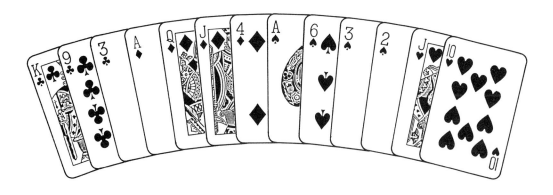

When you first pick up your cards, arrange them like this avoiding adjacent suits of the same colour, for example, with clubs on the far left, followed by diamonds, spades, and hearts on the far right, in descending order of face value.

The two phases of Bridge

At last you are ready to play bridge. But no, we will not let you start yet. The game has two principal phases–**Bidding** and **Play.** Bidding precedes the play but will mean little to a novice until we have described what happens in the play. So we recommend some play first, and will return to the matter of bidding later. The rules for the play of the cards are similar to whist, a fore-runner of bridge, so it eases you into bridge if we start by playing a little whist.

The first trick

One player, (for the moment let us select the player on dealer's left for the honour), chooses any card from his hand and places it face upwards on the table. We are going to play one TRICK of this deal. A trick consists of one card contributed by each of the four players following in clockwise rotation round to the left from the player who LED to the trick. The card led to the trick determines the suit of the trick, i.e. if a heart is led, it is a heart trick; if a club was led, a club trick. The person to the leader's left plays next by selecting a card from his hand and placing it face upwards on the table. If possible, this must be a card of the same suit. The requirement to FOLLOW SUIT is a fundamental LAW of the game. If the player has no card of the suit led (i.e. he is VOID of that suit), he may play any card from his hand. This is called a DISCARD. When all four players have contributed one card each in rotation (each player following the suit led where possible), the four cards are inspected to see which player has won the trick. The highest card played, of the suit which was led to the trick, wins the trick.

Example: West leads the four of diamonds, North plays the ten of diamonds, East plays the queen of spades, and South the two of diamonds. Who wins the trick and what else can you deduce?

Answer: North won the trick. East has no diamonds left. If East later on is found to have had a diamond, he is said to have **revoked,** and the Laws lay down a penalty for his failure to follow suit, which may be as much as conceding two extra tricks to the opponents at the end of the play. To prevent too much damage occuring, the 1981 Laws of Rubber Bridge permit the partner of the player who does not follow suit to say 'Having no ... (diamonds)?', which gives the offender a chance to correct his error with a lesser penalty.

   The player who won the trick gathers the four cards together into a small pile and places them face downwards for his side. The player who won the trick must lead to the next trick, and may lead any card in his hand. You can keep going now for all thirteen tricks, which make up the play of one deal. Remember that the players facing each other are partners. Stack the tricks of a partnership together,

slightly overlapping to distinguish them, thus:

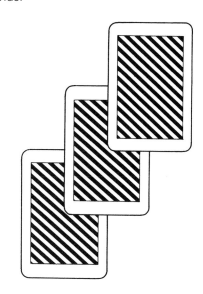

Because players 'North' and 'South' are partners, and players 'East' and 'West' are partners, stack the tricks won by each partnership together.

At the end of play count the number of tricks won by each side. For the moment, let us congratulate the side which wins the most tricks, i.e. more than six, as the winner. To make a GRAND SLAM at bridge one side must take all thirteen tricks, which you can see is difficult.

   For the next deal, repeat the same procedure, remembering that the task of dealing passes round the table, clockwise to the left.

Points to note

So far we have only described the mechanics of the play but it is not too early to appreciate something of the skill of the game. It is clearly helpful to remember what cards have gone, but do not worry if you find that very difficult.

Memory comes with practice and motivation. A cricketer who might absent-mindedly leave his bat in the pavilion can quote the last twenty Test centuries on a June Thursday at Lord's. It is the same with bridge. Once you play regularly, your memory will automatically improve. When you are a beginner it is more important to start making a few deductions and inferences.

Example: You lead a king and it wins the trick, even though the ace is out. You infer that your partner has the ace, because an opponent with the ace would probably have beaten your king.

When you cannot follow suit, dispose of a card which you do not need for winning later tricks. When your partner looks to be winning a trick do not waste your high cards on the same trick.

Trumps

Play a couple of deals as already described until you are confident about the mechanics of the lead, following suit, and winning tricks. Then introduce the matter of a TRUMP suit. At both whist and bridge for the play of one deal a particular suit may be given temporary preference over the other three. This is the trump suit. A trick is still won by the highest card of the suit led to a trick, *unless* a trump is played, in which case the highest trump played to the trick wins the trick. You must still follow suit if possible. If, however, you are void of the suit led, you may play a trump (also called RUFFING), or, of course, any other card.

Example: Clubs are trumps. West leads the king of spades, North plays the ace of spades, East the two of clubs, and South

the three of clubs. East and South must both be out of spades, and South wins the trick.

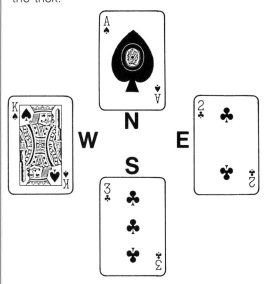

In bridge the trump suit is determined by the bidding, in whist it is called out before the deal is made. So finish your few deals of whist by playing with a different trump suit each time: clubs first, then diamonds, then hearts, then spades, and finally with NO-TRUMPS. Yes, that is what you were playing before you knew what a trump was.

Note that the side with most trumps has an advantage. The more the better. As the play progresses players run out of cards in one suit and have the opportunity to ruff.

You have now finished with whist and we can progress to bridge.

Zia Mahmood of Pakistan and London, won the 1990 Omar Sharif Individual held in Atlantic City, USA. The first prize of $40,000 was the highest in tournament bridge.

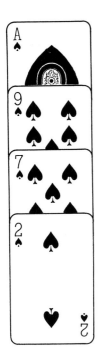

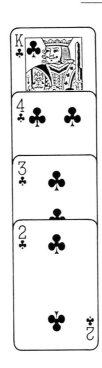

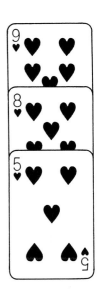

Dummy is arranged in rows of suits. If spades are trumps, for example, they are put on the right of the dummy hand, i.e. on the left as seen from across the table by dummy's partner, the 'declarer'.

THE · PLAY

The main difference between bridge and whist in the play is that, in bridge, one hand is placed face upwards on the table for all the players to see. The cards to be played by this seen hand are nominated, not by the owner of the hand, but by his partner. The seen hand is therefore called the DUMMY. The owner of the hand must only play cards as instructed by his partner, called the **declarer**. The declarer has to determine what cards are to be played by dummy, as well as what cards are to be played from his own hand, but in other respects the dummy hand obeys the usual rules–the dummy plays in normal rotation and if dummy wins the trick, dummy must lead to the next trick.

The contract

The bidding determines who is declarer,

and therefore who is dummy. The bidding results in the declarer having a **contract** for his side (i.e. declarer and dummy together) to make at least a certain number of tricks (always more than six), with a particular suit as trumps. For example, declarer's contract might be to make at least ten tricks (i.e. four more than the basic 'book' of six) with hearts as trumps. This contract would be named in the bidding as Four Hearts. Thus the long-winded statement: 'When it comes to the play, I and my partner between us will make at least three tricks more than the book of six provided clubs are trumps' would be shortened to the bid 'Three Clubs'. The final bid in the auction becomes the contract, and the partnership naming the contract becomes the declaring side. The contract consists of a **Level** (the number of tricks over six to be made) and a **Denomination** (what is to be trumps, including the possibility of **No-trumps**). The declarer is whichever member of the declaring side first suggested the final denomination (i.e. it may not be the member who named the final contract). The player to the left of declarer leads to the first trick. After the initial lead is made the dummy is faced. Dummy places his cards in columns of one suit each with the smaller cards nearer to declarer. If there is a trump suit it must be placed on dummy's right, i.e. declarer's left. So if spades were trumps, dummy might look something like the diagram. (left).

As we have not done any bidding yet, as an exercise, play enough practice deals to give each player a chance to be declarer. If you have a teacher, or a bridge-playing friend nearby, they can give you a realistic contract. Otherwise, simply put one hand down as dummy, allow declarer to say what he wants to have as trumps, and give him the chance to make as many tricks as possible. If you have a contract you will be able to check whether it has been fulfilled at the end of play. The side opposing declarer are called the DEFENDERS. Their objective is to win sufficient tricks to prevent declarer making the contract.

Example The contract is Three Notrumps. How many tricks must the defence obtain to defeat the contract?

Answer At least five. (Remember that the contract says how many tricks more than six declarer must make–his target was therefore nine of the thirteen tricks. If the defence make at least five, declarer must have been held to eight or less).

Handling a dummy is a very confusing matter at first, as declarer is in charge of two separate hands–even experienced players sometimes lead from the wrong hand. Remember, if dummy wins the trick,

dummy must lead to the next trick. However, the mechanics should soon become familiar, and give you a chance to start thinking about some of the skills of the game.

Do you suppose that the exposure of dummy makes bridge an easier game than whist? In fact it allows a bridge-player much more scope for skill in the play. Each player can see two hands–his own concealed hand, and the dummy hand. There are only two unseen hands and therefore only two places for any unseen card to be. A key skill in play is the ability to deduce where the unseen cards lie. For example, if the ace of hearts is not in your own hand, and not in dummy, and you have a clue that it is not with a third player, then it must lie with the fourth person. When one of the hands you cannot see fails to follow suit, all the remaining unseen cards in that suit must lie in the other concealed hand. And so, as the play progresses, a player can hope to build a mental picture of the unseen hands. If you manage it with confidence you are close to international standard. So don't expect this to be easy in the first few years!

We can now look at the bidding phase of bridge, but first a look over the points already learned:

SUMMARY

1. Contract bridge is a partnership game, North-South against East-West. At rubber bridge you cut for partners, the higher two cards playing together.

2. The player who draws the highest card has choice of seats (and deck of cards), and will deal the first hand. The left of dealer shuffles, the right of dealer cuts the deck, dealer deals one card at a time in clockwise rotation, starting with the player to the left.

3. When the deal is complete the players inspect their hands and then the bidding (or auction) takes place. The auction concludes by determining a contract, and one of the players as declarer of the contract.

4. The player to declarer's left leads to the first trick. The partner of declarer then places his hand face upwards on the table as dummy. Declarer determines what cards are played from the dummy, as well as deciding what cards are played from his own hand.

5. Each trick consists of four cards, one contributed by each hand in clockwise rotation round the table. The players must follow the suit of the card led to the trick, otherwise they may play any card in their hand. The highest card played to the trick, of the suit led, wins the trick, unless the contract specified a trump suit and a trump has been played to the trick, in which case the highest trump played to the trick wins the

trick. The player who wins a trick must lead to the next trick, but may play any card from his hand.

6. At the conclusion of a trick the four cards are stacked in a pile face downwards by the side that won the trick. At the conclusion of the hand thirteen tricks will have been played. The number of tricks won by declarer is compared with his contract to determine whether the contract has been fulfilled, or whether it was defeated.

BIDDING

The auction precedes the play but it will be easier to understand now you know the objective. The players call in rotation starting with the dealer and going round the table to the left. The player whose turn it is to call may either name a contract (e.g. 'Three Hearts') or say 'No Bid' (this is the same as saying 'Pass', which is the popular wording in most of the world, but we will stick with 'No Bid' which is more common in Britain). In addition there are two calls (Double and Redouble) which affect the scoring but do not change the contract.

Each contract named must specify the Level (the number of tricks over six the partnership contracts to take in the play), and the Denomination (what is to be trumps). The maximum number of tricks you can take is thirteen, so the maximum level of contract is seven (seven more than six equals all thirteen). How many different denominations do you think there are? The answer is *five* (clubs as trumps, diamonds, hearts, spades, and . . . no-trumps). As a contract may consist of any level put with any denomination (e.g. 'Four Spades'), how many different possible contracts are there? *Right*, the answer is 35 (7 levels multiplied by 5

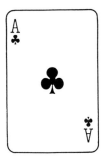    

Remember that there are five denominations when you are bidding, not just four: clubs, diamonds, hearts, spades – and no trumps.

denominations). The only calls permitted in the auction are these 35 bids, plus the common call of 'No Bid', and maybe 'Double' or 'Redouble'. Furthermore, each contract named must be senior to the previous contract named. 'Senior' means *either* that the level must be higher, *or*, if the level is the same, that the denomination is a higher ranking one (remember, the junior denomination is clubs, then diamonds, hearts, spades, ending with no-trumps as the senior).

So, if the dealer 'opened the bidding' by saying 'One Heart' – the next player to bid would not be permitted to say 'One Club' or 'One Diamond' but he could say 'One Spade' or 'Two Clubs', or, for that matter, 'Five Clubs'.

Why should a player name a higher contract than he needs to? The answer is that the scoring progressively rewards more ambitious contracts, provided, of course, that if they become the final contract, they are fulfilled in the play. So the main skill in bidding is to judge the highest scoring contract which your side can fulfil in the play. The problem is that this is a target for you and your partner

together, and you can only see one of the two hands!

The auction continues round and round until three consecutive players say 'No Bid'. The auction then ends, the final bid becomes the contract, and the declarer is the member of the declaring side who first named the denomination of the contract. The player on declarer's left leads to the first trick. Dummy is then faced and the play commences.

You therefore have two quite separate problems to solve during the auction; namely, how many tricks to go for, and what to have as trumps. The level of the contract will mainly be determined by the combined trick-taking potential of the two hands, a characteristic which is called the **Strength** of the hand.

The choice of trump suit is mainly determined by the *number* of cards in each suit that the partners have together (in general, the more trumps the partnership has, the better)–this characteristic is called the **Shape** of the hand.

If only you knew your partner's strength and shape you could readily judge the best contract for your side. How can you deduce this without seeing his hand? *Answer:* by making inferences from the bids that he makes. Take this simple example. Your partner is dealer and says 'One Heart'. With the knowledge you have so far, what deduction about his hand would you make?

Take 'shape' first: this means the distribution of different suits in his hand. The right conclusion to draw is that your partner has no suit with more cards in it than he has in hearts (otherwise he would have suggested that other suit first as trumps). He must therefore have at least four hearts. (A bridge hand has 13 cards, and at most four suits, so at least one of the suits must contain at least four cards.)

Now consider strength. A fair deduction is that the strength of his hand must be better than average, for he is stating that he expects the partnership to take more than half the tricks. We need to be much more precise than this, however. For a partnership to be happy with a suit as trumps, they need to have more of that suit than their opponents. If your side has seven cards in a suit, the other side will have six, which is a negligible advantage. So the normal target for selecting trumps is to find a suit in which you and partner together have at least eight cards. One of the two partners must therefore have at least four cards in the suit, and we can recommend that a player does not suggest a suit as trumps unless he has at least four cards in the suit. If the partner, by chance, also had four or more, he would know the side had located a 'fit' of at least eight cards, making a satisfactory trump suit. If not, he could suggest a different trump suit until the side found a fit, or chose to have notrumps.

To assess the *strength* of their hand, bridge-players use a numerical method ('the point count'). By making inferences from the bidding about partner's point count, it is possible to assess the

partnership's trick-taking potential and therefore the appropriate level for the final contract. Different players might prefer different methods of assessing strength but, fortunately, one method has become by far the most popular and this is the one we now describe.

Counting Your Points

There are three main elements which affect the trick-taking potential of a hand. (a) the high cards, which win tricks by sheer power of rank; (b) the long suits which win tricks because, late in the play, the opponents have no cards left in the suit; and, curiously enough, on occasion, (c) very short suits. How can a short suit be of value? *Answer:* when a hand becomes void of a suit which is not trumps, the hand is able to trump a lead of that suit and so win a trick.

(a) High Card Points The universally popular method is to count 4 for an ace, 3 for a king, 2 for a queen, 1 for a jack, and ignore the smaller cards. The pack therefore contains 40 high card points, and the average hand contains 10 high card points (the 40 points are divided amongst 4 players). Also, as there are thirteen tricks to be won, you can see that, roughly, each extra 3 points a side holds, should enable it to make an extra trick in the play (40 divided by 13 equals 3).

(b) Long Suits The most popular method is to add one point for each card in excess of four in any one suit, i.e. 1 point for a 5 card suit, 2 points for a 6 card suit, and 1 point each for two 5 card suits.

(c) Short Suits The most popular method is to assess a 2 card suit (a DOUBLETON) as worth 1 point, a 1 card suit (SINGLETON) as 2 points and a no-card suit (VOID) as 3 points. There is a snag,

4 points   *3 points*   *2 points*   *1 point*

How good (strong) is your hand? The first and most important thing to do is to count your high card points. Add up the worth of all the jacks, queens, kings and aces in your hand, according to the values shown.

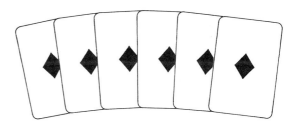

5 cards – plus 1 point   *6 cards – plus 2 points*

Long suits – that is, suits in which you have more than four cards – also add to the points strength of your hand, as shown.

doubleton (2 cards) – plus 1 point

Singleton (1 card) – plus 2 points

Void (no cards in a suit) – plus 3 points

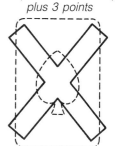

Short suits – that is, suits in which you have only two cards, one card, or no cards at all – also have a points value, as shown. But beware! If you don't find an eight-card fit with your partner, you should not add on these points, because you will probably be overestimating the strength of your hand.

however. If the final contract is no-trumps, a short suit is bad news–worse, if your partner insists that the short suit becomes trumps, the shortness is of negative value! In this book we recommend that you only add on the value of the short suits when you know your side has a trump fit of at least 8 cards.

Exercise in Counting Points

There is an exercise for four novice bridge-players which is both fun and educational, and requires no knowledge of real bidding. Each player counts his points (adding together high cards, long suits, and short suit values). Then, starting bidding with the dealer, go round the table to the left, allowing each person the option of saying how many points they hold or 'No Bid' if they do not wish to do so. The contract will be played by the side with most points (if equal, by the first to 'open') and declarer will be the player of that side with most points (if equal, the first to 'open'). You are advised to 'open' for your side if you have 13 points or

more and 'respond' to your partner's opening if you think your side has the most points. The 'bidding' ends with three consecutive 'No Bids'. The level of the contract (i.e. the number of tricks declarer has to make) is the partnership points divided by 3, and declarer can choose trumps after he has seen dummy. (Sound advice is to choose the suit with most cards between the two hands. If your side has no suit with more than seven cards, choose notrumps). You will find this exercise gives you a highly realistic contract and will teach you to think of the two hands as working together. You will also begin to see the problem of real bidding where you have to select the best final contract with only the sight of one hand and clues from the auction to assist you. Consider this example:
Dealer: West

West	**North**	**East**	**South**
No bid	15	No bid	9
No bid	No bid	No bid	

North is declarer and has to make 8 tricks (15 + 9 divided by 3). West should have less than 13 points as he did not "open".

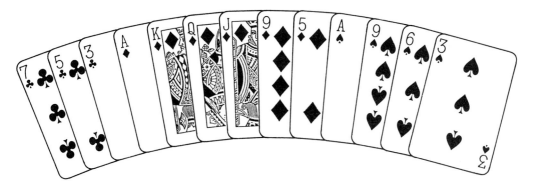

How many points does this hand have –
which is the same as asking how strong is
it? First, count the high cards: there are
five of them, and their points value adds
up to 14. The hand also has a long suit –
six diamond cards, which is valued at
another 2 points. If, during the bidding,
you find that you have a 'fit' with your
partner of eight cards in one suit –
probably diamonds in this case – you can
add another 3 points for the 'void' (i.e.
having no cards) in hearts. This makes a
total of 19 points. Feeling dizzy yet with all
this calculation? Don't worry – one thing
you can be sure of, you have a strong
hand here!

Partnership Agreements and Bidding Systems

It is easier to assess the best contract if you can make precise inferences from your partner's calls. The Laws of Bridge permit you to agree with partner precise meanings to be taken from your bids but the Laws state that such agreements must not be secret–the opponents are entitled to know them too. For example, in many countries, though not in Britain, it is popular to agree that an opening bid of one of the two higher ranking suits (hearts and spades) will guarantee at least *five* cards in the suit named. A comprehensive list of your agreements is called your 'system' of bidding. Designing a good system takes years of experimentation . . . don't try it yourself until you are close to international standard!.

In Britain, the most popular system is called ACOL, named after the road in Hampstead where the bridge club of the inventors was. (One of the four devisers of ACOL, Iain McCleod, went on to become Chancellor of the Exchequer.) The bidding methods recommended in this book are based on the ACOL system.

Opening the Bidding

The moment you have sorted your cards, count your high card points, and your long suit points and add these together. We recommend you do not assess your short suit values until you locate a suitable trump suit: you will then upgrade the value of your hand.

The auction starts with dealer. If he has less than 13 points we advise 'No Bid'. With 13 to 19 points he should open the bidding with One of his longest suit. What suit should you open if you happen to have two suits of equal length? This is a complex matter, for the 'best' suit to open will depend on how the bidding progresses. You have to anticipate your

Andy Robson was a member of the British team that won the 1991 European Championships. He was world juniors champion in 1989. (See page 72).

later bids as well! More advanced books will give chapters of advice. We suggest a very simple rule for novices: with two 5 card suits, mention first the *higher* ranking (you hope to tell partner on the next round about the lower ranking one); with suits of only four cards, start with the *lower* ranking (on the next round you may re-bid in your second suit: or, if that would take the level too high, suggest no-trumps).

Exploratory Bidding

The principal objective when seeking a trump suit is to keep the bidding low–your side wants to find a trump suit of eight cards before the level of the auction exceeds your ability to fulfil the contract. This type of bidding is called *exploratory* bidding. Here is an example with West as dealer:

West	North	East	South
1♥	1♠	2♣	No bid
2♦	No bid	3♦	No bid
No bid	No bid		

What can we deduce from this auction?

1♥: West has 13 to 19 points and no suit longer than hearts.
1♠: North's longest suit is spades and

he also has the strength to enter the auction for his side.

2♣: East knows West has at least 13 points and can 'respond' with much less strength than 13 points. East does not have four hearts and so suggests a new trump suit, clubs, his longest. As clubs are lower ranking than spades he has to raise the level. South, with a poor hand, passes.

2♦: West is obliged to bid again because both partners are seeking a trump suit and East may have a good hand. West does not have four clubs and tells East about his second suit, diamonds.

3♦: Eureka! East also has four diamonds and 'raises' the suit to indicate the partnership has located an eight card trump fit. West, who has a minimum opening bid, decides the level of contract has gone high enough and passes. Three consecutive 'No Bids' end the auction. The final bid of Three Diamonds becomes the contract. West, who first named diamonds as trumps, is the declarer. North has to lead, and East will then place his hand face upwards on the table, as dummy. The side will only obtain a plus score if the contract is fulfilled, which means West must win nine tricks or more.

When players name a trump suit which has not previously been suggested, they are exploring and the main purpose is to show the *shape* of their hand; by contrast, their *strength* is not well defined. In the example already given the shape of West and East might be:

West	East
♠ x x x	♠ x x x
♥ x x x x x	♥ x
♦ x x x x	♦ x x x x
♣ x	♣ x x x x x

(The x's indicate the number of cards in each suit).

Note that West's longest suit is hearts, East's longest suit is clubs, but the partnership's longest suit is diamonds. Only by describing their shape can they discover this.

But bidding the right contract also requires you to assess strength. There is a completely different sort of bidding, called LIMIT bidding, in which players describe their strength accurately.

Limit Bidding

Look at this example auction. North and South Pass throughout so we can just show the calls of West and East:

West	East
1♥	3♥
4♥	No bid

West opens 1♥, promising 13 to 19 points and no suit longer than hearts. East, who happens to have at least four hearts, at once knows the partnership has an eight card fit, and a satisfactory trump suit. He indicates this by raising West's suit, as high as the strength of his hand justifies.

How did he decide to bid Three Hearts rather than Two or Four? First, he upgraded the value of his hand by adding points for his short suits; next, he made the cautious assumption that West had a minimum opening bid of 13 points; finally, having made that cautious assumption he bid as boldly as he dared, with a direct relationship between the points he held and the level bid.

We know that each additional 3 points is worth one extra trick to a side, but experience shows that, in a trump contract, declarer usually does a trick better than you might expect (it is an advantage to control two hands in the play). Most players reckon that 24 points will produce 9 tricks, 27 points will produce 10 tricks; 33 points will be enough for 12 tricks (the small slam), and 36 points sufficient for a grand slam. West has a minimum of 13 points. So if East held 8 points, East would be happy to try for a contract of 8 tricks; with 11 points he would bid for 9 tricks; with 14 points for 10 tricks, and so on. Of course, East has to make the same call if he has a point more, or a point less than the exact appropriate number, so we say that East's raise to Three Hearts shows 10 to 12 points. With 13 to 15 points he would have raised to Four Hearts. With 7 to 9 points he would have raised to Two Hearts. With less he should be disinclined to bid at all, but there is a disadvantage in passing so it is widely accepted that the range for a minimum raise is actually 6 to 9 points. Responder, with 0 to 5, will pass.

So we have well specified ranges for a limit bid: namely 6–9, 10–12, 13–15, 16–18 etc. Each extra level bid promises one extra trick (remember, 3 points is equivalent to one trick).

Reaching the right level is not finished, however, by East's limit bid of Three Hearts. East based his call on the cautious assumption that West had only 13 points. If West actually has more he can justify raising the level further. West can upgrade his hand (adding short suit points because a trump fit has been found) and every spare 3 points will justify one extra trick. For example, if two partners bid: One Spade–Two Spades–Four Spades–No bid, how strong are they? Answer: the first call (exploratory) showed 13 to 19 points, the second was a minimum raise (6 to 9), and opener's final call showed he actually had 19 points (6 more than minimum and therefore worth two extra tricks).

The actual objective in bidding is to

reach the contract that will produce the best score for your side. As yet, we have not mentioned scoring. There is a good reason for this. Bridge scoring is complicated at first sight and the main skill you need in bidding (judging the highest contract your side can make) can be practised enjoyably without the chore of scoring. However, we cannot avoid the matter any longer.

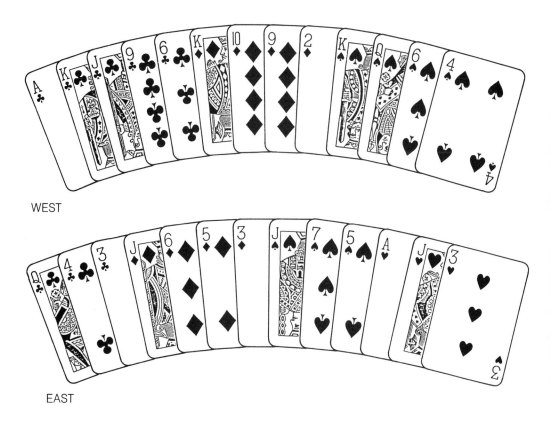

WEST

EAST

How many points does this partnership have? And how many tricks should it expect to win? If the partners can find out through the bidding that they have a fit of eight cards between them in clubs, then West can assume that his hand is strengthened by his void in hearts – another 3 points. West then has 20 points – remember an extra point for the long five-card suit – and East has 9 points. This total of 29 points should be good enough for at least 10 tricks: that is, a contract of four clubs, or possibly five.

SCORING

Bridge scoring, though complicated, is beautifully designed to balance risk and reward. The higher the contract, the greater the risk of failure, but the higher will be the reward for success. The side with the good cards is tempted into bidding for the most ambitious contract it can manage. The defenders, the side with fewer resources, will have a smaller objective in defeating the contract. (To beat a grand slam, the defence only has to make one trick.) Accurate bidding will make the play a close run affair. That is why contract bridge immediately became more popular than auction bridge or whist, where a side has no reason to set itself an ambitious target.

This is the basics of scoring for Rubber bridge: a 'rubber' is a contest to win two games ... and a side makes a game when the trick value of their contracts bid and made equals 100 points or more. There is a major bonus for being the first side to win two games. So we start by defining the value of the contracts, then specify the value of overtricks (tricks made in excess of contract), mention the bonuses for making two games, or for succeeding in a slam, and then the penalties for failing in a contract.

A score-card is divided into quadrants, looking like this:

We	They

In the left hand column record plus points for our side (achieved if we make a contract or the opponents fail); in the right hand column record minus points (if our contract fails, or theirs succeeds). Below the horizontal line record points for contracts bid and made so that you know when a game has been made. Put all other points above the line. At the end of the rubber add up the two columns and take the difference to work out the winning margin. If you want to play for money you would agree a stake 'per hundred points' but we do not advise this for beginners. (Nevertheless, at a 'penny a hundred', a typical rubber would only cost the losers about 10 pence – not too painful!)

The trick value of contracts is as follows:

For clubs or diamonds (the minor suits):
    20 per trick named
For hearts or spades (the major suits):
    30 per trick named
For no-trumps:
    10 more than ♥'s or ♠'s
(that is the same as saying 40 for the first, and 30 thereafter).

By trick 'named' we mean the level named in the contract. So the value of the contract Four Clubs is 80 points even though you must make ten tricks to succeed. The value of Two Spades is 60

points, and the value of Two No-trumps 70 points.

If a contract succeeds put this value *below the line* for the side that made the contract, e.g. if on the first deal of a rubber we bid Three Clubs, making just nine tricks, our score-card looks like this:

We	They
60	

If a side makes more tricks than they bid for, the value of the over-tricks (20 per trick for a minor, 30 for hearts, spades or no-trumps) is recorded 'above the line' because overtricks do not assist in making game. If, on the second deal, they bid

Three Hearts and made ten tricks, our score-card would show:

We	They
	30
60	90

They have '90 below' for making Three Hearts, and '30 above' for the overtrick. (Traditionally we put scores near the line and work outwards as the scores build up.)

On the next deal suppose we bid Two No-trumps and make nine tricks, the score-card would look like this:

We	They
30	30
60	90
70	

We now have 130 points 'below the line'. As this is equal to or greater than 100, we have made a game. To indicate this a fresh line is drawn below, and points for the second game will go below this new line, i.e. the score-card now shows:

We	They
30	30
60	90
70	

All the points shown will be added up at the end of the Rubber. The opponents have not lost their 90 points but they are now above the line–it will not help them in the new game, which begins all square.

A game can be, and usually is, bid and made in one deal. Can you work out the game contracts? They are Five Diamonds (20x5=100), Five Clubs, Four Spades (30x4=120), Four Hearts, and Three No-trumps (40+30+30=100). Anything less than a game is called a partscore. The most important aspect of bidding is to bid and make your game contracts when you can. Slams, though highly rewarding, are relatively infrequent.

If on the next deal we bid and make Four Hearts we would have a second game. The rubber would be over and there is a bonus of 700 points for winning

by two games to nil. (The bonus for winning 2–1 is 500.) The final score-card looks like this:

We	They
700	
30	30
60	90
70	
120	
980	120

We won by 860 which, at a penny a hundred, would mean the winner received nine pence from the opponent on his left.

In this imaginary rubber every contract succeeded. Real life is not like that. If a contract fails there is a penalty to be awarded to the defenders. The value and denomination of the failed contract is irrelevant. What matters is the number of tricks by which it failed (the 'undertricks') and whether declarer already had a game or not. This last factor arises to balance risk and reward. The reward for a second game is the rubber bonus, so the scoring makes the penalties for failure twice as great once a side already has one game. The side with a game is said to be 'Vulnerable'; a side which has not scored a game is 'Non-vulnerable'. The penalty

for failure non-vulnerable is 50 per under-trick, irrespective of the contract, and this is increased to 100 per under-trick when vulnerable. This penalty goes above the line on the defenders' side of the score-card.

Slam Bonuses

If you achieve the satisfaction of bidding and making a small slam (12 tricks) or grand slam (13 tricks), in addition to the trick value, and the game, you are also awarded one of these bonuses:

	Non-vulnerable	Vulnerable
Small slam	500	750
Grand slam	1000	1500

Honour Bonuses

Rubber bridge has a few 'fun' (I think, silly) bonuses: any player holding all five honours (AKQJ10) in the trump suit, or all 4 aces in a no-trump contract can claim a bonus of 150 points. A player with four out of five trump honours can claim a bonus of 100 points. All bonuses go above the line.

Christian Mari has won two world titles for France. Mari won one of the first televised bridge tournaments in Britain.

Doubling and Redoubling

There is a further complication. In the auction, a contract may be doubled by an opponent. If the doubled contract becomes the final one, the contract remains unchanged but its value is doubled. As the reward for success and the penalty for failure are both increased, an opponent will only wish to double a final contract which he expects to fail. If the declaring side are sure, however, of its success either may redouble, effectively upping the stakes again. These are relatively rare events so we suggest you simply look up the score when it arises. These are summarized in the scoring tables shown below:

SCORING · TABLES

Contracts which Succeed
Trick score (Below the Line)

	♣ ♦	♥ ♠	No Trumps	
			1st	Thereafter
Undoubled	20	30	40	30
Doubled	40	60	80	60
Redoubled	80	120	160	120

Overtricks (above the Line)

	Non-vulnerable	Vulnerable
Undoubled	Trick value	Trick value
Doubled	100	200
Redoubled	200	400

In addition, the side succeeding in making a contract which is doubled or redoubled is given a bonus of 50 above the line 'for the insult' of being doubled!

Contracts Which Fail
Penalty (Above the Line to the
Defenders)
Undertricks

Not Vulnerable

	Undoubled	Doubled	Redoubled
For first undertrick	50	100	200
For each additional undertrick	50	200	400

Vulnerable

	Undoubled	Doubled	Redoubled
For first undertrick	100	200	400
For each additional undertrick	100	300	600

Bonus Points

For winning the Rubber 2–0	700
For winning the Rubber 2–1	500
Holding the Honours (A K Q J 10) in Trump Suit	150
Holding any four Honours in Trump Suit	100
Holding four aces when contract in No Trumps	150
Making a Grand Slam (13 tricks)	1000 (not vulnerable) 1500 (if vulnerable)
Making a Small Slam (12 tricks)	500 (not vulnerable) 750 (if vulnerable)

We warned you that bridge scoring was complicated! Start by knowing the trick values, game contracts, and the penalties for undoubled under-tricks; look up the others as they arise. With your knowledge of scoring we can now say more about bidding.

Bidding No-trumps

The usual reason for bidding no-trumps is either that the player making the bid has no particular preference for suggesting a trump suit, or that the partnership has been unable to locate a trump suit of 8 cards. You can now see a further reason: no-trumps scores more and, in particular, game is Three No-trumps (i.e.nine tricks) instead of, say, Five Clubs. However, you will find no-trump contracts more difficult to make because the defenders have the big advantage of the opening lead. They will select their longest suit which may strike your weak spot. Most players reckon that you need 25 or 26 points (and you count nothing for short suits) when trying for Three No-trumps, whereas 9 tricks in a suit contract requires only 24 points (inclusive of short-suit points). So it is just as well that, as no-trumps is the senior denomination, you can keep the bidding a level lower than would be the case when raising partner. All no-trump bids are limit bids (i.e. they define the strength of your hand to within one trick), so this is the scheme of responses to an opening bid of one of a suit:

(a) The response of One No-trump shows a balanced hand of 6–9 points with less than four cards in opener's suit.

(b) The response of 2 No-trumps shows 10–12 points.

(c) Three No-trumps shows 13–15 points.

Players often respond One No-trump on hands which are not really balanced, because the alternative action (of suggesting a new trump suit) would take the auction to a higher level. Immediate responses of Two or Three No-trumps, however, suggest a very balanced hand, because you could have explored for a trump suit at a lower level. The most balanced hand shape is 4-3-3-3, but 4-4-3-2 is more common (where partner opened in one of the shorter suits).

The Opening One No-Trump

All no-trump bids are limit bids and the opening bid of one no-trump also shows a balanced hand (i.e.4-3—3-3 or 4-4—3-2) in shape.. However, we have to admit that there is an unresolved debate amongst the experts about the best strength for the opening. As we are following a scheme where the limit ranges are 6–9, 10–12, 13–15, 16–18 and an opening bid

What do you do when you have a balanced hand like this, and it's your turn to open the bidding? You have the required number of points to bid, but they are shared out among all the suits. The best bid for the beginner is 'One-No-trump'. It promises your partner that you have 13 to 15 points, and tells him or her immediately that you have a balanced hand.

promises at least 13 points, we might say that the opening One No-trump showed 13–15 points (the 'weak' no-trump) or, instead, 16–18 points (the 'strong' no-trump). The strong no-trump is very popular in America and France, but in Britain the weak no-trump has more adherents so we will stick with that. (Many British tournament players like to use a range of 12–14.)

The weak no-trump has one major advantage of particular benefit to beginners. The most difficult hand on which to find a rebid is the minimum balanced opening. If you open the hand 'One No-trump' your problems of description are solved, for your partner has a very accurate picture of your hand. With an unbalanced hand, or a stronger balanced hand, you open One of your longest suit and have no problem finding a rebid.

The strong no-trumpers have such severe difficulties in finding a rebid with a balanced 13 points that they often open One Club on such a hand even when clubs is not their longest suit. This is called using a 'prepared' One Club (i.e. preparing to *rebid* One No-trump). This is the argument in favour of the weak no-trump but, of course, the debate would not have raged since bridge began, if there was not another case to put. If you open a weak no-trump and partner has a bad hand you will be in a poor contract. We specify that, if partner responds in a suit at the Two level, he is *not* exploring but merely selecting a final contract which he believes will be superior to One No-trump. Responder makes this 'weakness take-out' whenever he has a five card suit or longer and no hope of game.

Please try the weak no-trump style but, be warned. If you join a bridge game, the first matter to be resolved with a partner you don't know is: 'What strength of opening no-trump do you like?' – and some partners will be quite insistent that you play their style. That is why we have explained the strong no-trump as well.

OTHER · OPENINGS

With only 5 points, responder will pass an opening bid at the one level. 25 points can be enough for game. So, a player with 20 points or more will wish to make a stronger bid than the normal One bid. In ACOL all the opening bids at the *Two level* are strong. The opening Two No-trumps is a limit bid showing 20–22 points and a balanced hand. An opening two bid in a suit has a wider range of strength and promises at least five cards in the suit named. (Later in this book we make special reference to the opening Two Clubs.) Some players like to define such a Two bid as promising eight tricks without assistance from their partner. You will find this definition is much the same as saying you have at least 20 points counting both high cards and points for shape.

♠ K4 ♥ AKQ 10 6 4 ♦ AK 8 6 ♣ 7
A typical hand with which you should open Two Hearts, using the ACOL system.

Opening at the Three level or higher

As an opening bid at the Two level shows a strong hand you might well wonder why anyone should wish to open with a higher bid. The answer is that the auction has *two* sides competing. The time to open high is when you have no desire to explore yourself but wish to stop the opponents entering the auction. Such a bid is called a pre-empt. If you have a decent seven card suit but as few as 6 to 9 high card points, it would be standard practice to open the bidding with Three of your long suit. If you have 10 high card points and a seven card suit (worth 3 points in shape) you have the values to justify opening at the One level.

The overcall

A player who enters the auction after the opponents have already opened is said to make an overcall. It is dangerous to do this on a balanced hand – so forget the weak no-trump in this situation. If you overcall with a bid of One No-trump you must have a balanced hand of 16–18 points including a trick in the suit named by the opponent. This 'stopper' prevents them running their long suit against you.

When you overcall with a suit bid, very different tactics are involved. To some extent it is more dangerous than opening, yet it is natural for any player to want to compete in the auction whenever possible. If you give the opponents a free run, they are much more likely to reach their best contract than if you put your oar in.

The tactic we recommend is this: when overcalling have the security of a suit which is at least five cards in length. Having said that, enter the auction on 3 points less than a normal opening if you can bid your suit at the One level. If your overcall has to be at the Two level you should have at least the values for an opening bid.

You may be wondering what to bid when you have a good hand which has no five card suit and no stopper in the opponent's suit. We promise to solve this problem for you later in the book.

One last bit of advice about overcalls. If you have a minimum opening bid (i.e. 13 to 15 points) and the opponent opens with a suit that also happens to be your best suit, say 'No bid'. The deal is probably a misfit (where neither side has a suitable trump suit). It may take the opponents some rounds of bidding to discover this, by which time they may have reached too high. The golden rule in competitive auctions is this: bid up when you have a good fit with partner, be cautious when you have the same suit as an opponent.

This advice completes our introduction to the game of bridge. We now answer some queries you may have about the Rules and then move to the matter of technique in bidding, play and defence.

The opponent on your right has opened the bidding with One Heart. You have enough points to enter the bidding, but you hold five heart cards. It's best to say 'No bid' and hope that your opponents get themselves in trouble by bidding too high, before they find out that they don't have a 'fit' in that suit.

RULES CLINIC

In this section we answer some of the queries the reader may have about the Laws of bridge. The Laws are complex because they have to specify what is to be done when something goes wrong, in every conceivable circumstance. When you begin to play the game seriously, you should purchase a copy of the Laws (see Useful Addresses) and refer to them when necessary. While you are a beginner it is often simpler just to correct the error without compensation to the injured side. The Laws do not try to 'punish' people for incorrect procedure, but they do try to ensure that the other side does not suffer in any way.

You said that the auction ends when three consecutive players have passed. So what happens if at the

(Previous page) American Big Business meets the House of Commons in a private bridge match at the London home of the late Malcolm Forbes. At the table from the left are: Laurence Tisch, head of CBS television; Michael Mates, MP, watching Sir Peter Emery, MP (Conservative), who partners Dr. John Marek (Labour MP for Wrexham), with back to camera. Malcolm Forbes is on the right. Standing, watching, between Emery and Forbes, is the author; next to him is Zia Mahmood (see page 23).

start of the auction, the first three players pass? Doesn't the fourth player have a chance?

Yes, you are right. All four players must have the opportunity to bid.

So what happens if all four players pass on the first round of the auction?

There is no contract and therefore no play. There is simply no score on the deal. The hands are thrown in and the right to deal goes to the next player in normal rotation.

What happens if a player calls when it is not his turn?

If the opponent on his left 'condones' the error by then calling, the auction simply keeps going. Usually, however, the mistake is spotted, the call out of turn is cancelled, and the bidding reverts to the person whose turn it was to call. As the partner of the one who called out of turn has gained some information to which he was not entitled, the Laws specify a penalty. The severity of this penalty depends on whether the call out of turn was a Pass or a bid, and whether the partner was due to call before or after the person who called out of turn. There could also be a lead penalty during the play. Novices may prefer to ignore the penalties and simply cancel the call out of turn, acting as if it had not occurred.

What happens if a player makes a bid which is lower than the previous contract named?

Again, the error would be condoned if the next player called. Usually, however, the mistake is spotted and the illegal bid is cancelled. The player concerned is given the choice of increasing the level of his bid, in the same denomination, to make it 'sufficient' (in which case there is no penalty); or of making any other legal bid or pass. If, however, he chooses this second option, the Laws specify a penalty–the partner must Pass for the remainder of the auction (and may suffer a lead penalty in the play).

Is a player allowed to double his partner's bid?

NO! Either *opponent* may double. When a legal double has been made, the auction keeps going until three consecutive players have passed. Any of the three players following the double may choose to bid (higher than the doubled bid, of course). This new bid is treated as not being doubled unless an opponent doubles this as well.
For example:

West	North	East	South
1♠	2♥	Double	3♦
No bid	No bid	Double	No bid
No bid	3♥	Double	No bid
No bid	No bid		

West opens and North overcalls. East, who has a good holding in hearts and enough values to realize North cannot make his contract, doubles. South, who has bad hearts and long diamonds, hopes to improve matters by changing the trump suit. West, who has only a minimum opening and poor diamonds, passes, leaving the decision to East. East has enough to be confident that Three Diamonds will fail as well, so he Doubles again. When this gets back to North he decides that it will be a disaster to play with diamonds as trumps and goes back to hearts. East gleefully Doubles again; South passes miserably, regretting his earlier 'Rescue' into diamonds. The contract is Three Hearts Doubled. Remember that the Double only affects the scoring, and does not change the contract–North has contracted to make nine tricks and his success or failure will be measured against that target.

If a doubled contract succeeds, can a contract which, undoubled, would not have been a game, now be worth a game?

Yes. The contract value is doubled and if that figure exceeds 100 the contract is worth a game, e.g. Two Hearts Doubled, if successful, scores a game
($60 \times 2 = 120$) but Two Diamonds Doubled does not ($40 \times 2 = 80$). When a game is scored in these circumstances the successful declarer is said to have been 'doubled into game'.

Similarly, can you be doubled into slam?

No! A slam is a contract to make 12 or 13 tricks, whereas game is a specific score. A double changes the score but not the contract, so you therefore cannot be doubled into slam.

When and who can redouble?

When a contract has been doubled, either member of the declaring side may redouble, at their turn to call. Redoubles are rare because the defender who doubled has indicated an expectation that the contract will fail. Once the redouble is made, all the other three players still have a chance to bid.

BRIDGE

What happens when the auction is finished, if the wrong defender leads to the first trick?

The Laws give declarer several options; for example, to accept or reject the lead out of turn. The penalty arises because the other defender has seen a card to which he was not entitled. Players are allowed to, indeed, advised to, acquire the habit of leading face downwards; only turning their card when the others indicate everything is alright. If they say, 'It's not your lead!' no harm has been done and there would be no penalty.

What happens during the play if declarer leads from the wrong hand?

No harm has been done, so the 1987 Laws of Duplicate Bridge simply allow the defenders to ask him to lead from the correct hand. In the 1981 Laws of Rubber Bridge he is also required to lead a card of the same suit if possible.

What happens when the wrong defender leads?

Some damage has been done because the other defender has seen a card to which he was not entitled. The Laws specify a penalty similar to the opening lead out of turn. Novices will usually permit the offender to retract the lead without penalty.

What happens if a player exposes a card inadvertently? (by dropping it, for example).

If *declarer* exposes a card, only the opponents have benefited so the card is simply replaced without penalty. If a defender drops a card, his partner has seen something to which he is not entitled, so there is a penalty. This depends on the circumstances but usually the exposed card has to be played at the first legal opportunity.

What happens if a player fails to follow suit when actually holding a card of the suit led?

This is called a REVOKE and it certainly disrupts the game, particularly as the error may not be discovered until much later. To prevent this happening the 1981 Laws permit players to enquire of a partner who does not follow suit: 'Having no ... (whatever suit was led)?' If the player discovers he has a card of the suit led *before* his side has played to the next trick, the mistake can be corrected and the card played in error becomes an exposed card. If the revoke is discovered *after* the offender's side has played to the next trick then there is a penalty. This may be a credit for the non-offending side of as much as two extra tricks at the end of play. However, if the offending side did not actually win any tricks from the revoke trick onwards, then no damage could have been done, and there would be no penalty.

What happens if a player's mannerism conveys information to his partner?

The main point of bridge is to make deductions from a specified set of clues, namely the sight of your own hand, and dummy, and the calls made and cards played by the others. You are also entitled to know what agreements the opponents have concerning the meaning conveyed by their calls. You are not entitled to any information from your partner other than the calls he makes, and the cards he plays.

To convey information deliberately to your partner by mannerism or, worse, secret signal, is cheating. Don't play with

N

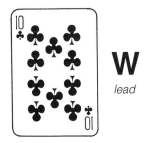

W

lead

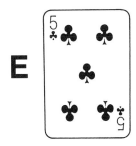

E

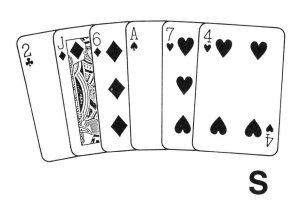

S

In this situation, spades are trumps, and West has led with the 10 of clubs. North and East have followed suit, playing clubs. South, however, in his haste to trump with a spade, had overlooked the 2 of clubs in his own hand, which he must play. This is a revoke, and is liable to a penalty.

someone who does this.

Quite frequently, however, players inadvertently, by their mannerism, give a clue to their hand. The most common is the hesitation while a player makes a decision. For example, West opens One Spade, North thinks for some time and then Passes. The other three players are all aware that North was wondering whether to bid. Bridge is a game of thought and such hesitations cannot be avoided. However, in such a situation, in order to encourage players to conceal their mannerisms whenever possible, the Laws give the opponents an advantage. The Law says that an opponent may make use of information so gained, but that partner must not. Imagine that following North's hesitation, East passes

and it is South's turn to call. If South has a clear cut bid he should make it, but, with a close decision, he should Pass. A player who makes inferences from his partner's mannerisms is said to be unethical, rather than a cheat. Of course, South may feel he has a clear cut bid when East or West think he does not. In tournament bridge, East or West could ask for a ruling from the Referee on whether South's decision was clear cut, without necessarily implying that South had been unethical. The Referee has powers to award an adjusted score and, when he is in doubt, will *give* the benefit to the side that avoided any mannerism. Thus it is in the players' own interest to avoid, whenever possible, mannerisms which give a clue to their hand.

Doris Fischer was a member of the Austrian team that won the 1991 Women's European Chanpionships held in Killarney.

TECHNIQUE OF BIDDING

The next section is all about techniques you can use when bidding, to give information to your partner and, ultimately, to reach the best contract. There are three principal types of bid: exploratory, limit and conventional. As we have not mentioned conventions before, let us define them first.

Conventions

A convention is a call which, by prior agreement with partner, conveys a meaning different from that expected by the opponents. The Laws permit such agreements provided they are not secret– the opponents must be made aware of the agreement too. Some players take a delight in having very complex agreements which are difficult (and tedious) to explain. In tournament bridge a restriction is put on this by 'licensing' conventions for use. In rubber bridge, social pressures prevent agreements becoming too complex. There are only six in common use and we will refer to these in a moment. How can you recognize that your partner's call is a convention? Only by remembering your prior agreement with him; a player who uses a convention

is not permitted to remind his partner of the prior agreement. If a call is not conventional it is easy to distinguish whether it is exploratory or limit: the first mention of a *suit* is exploratory, other bids (i.e. all no-trump bids and the mention of a suit which has already been mentioned) are limit bids.

Exploratory bids

Although their main purpose is to show shape, these can also indicate a wide range of strength. For example, the opening bid of a suit at the One level shows 13–19 points with no suit longer than the one named. A minimum response by partner in a new suit can be anywhere in the range 6 to 15 points. (With 16 points or more responder can jump one level in a new suit to alert the opener that a slam may be in prospect.) When opening the bidding, if you have two suits to bid of unequal length, start with the longer. There are exceptions to this rule but if you put *quantity* before *quality* you will not go far wrong. When your two (or even three) suits are equal in length use the tip mentioned in the Game Guide (start with the higher ranking of two five card suits, but the lower ranking of four card suits).

The exploratory response

Respond to an opening suit bid with 6 points or more. If you have a reasonable alternative, avoid responding at the two level with less than 10 points. With two four-card suits to bid, show the first available. For example, imagine you hold four diamonds and four spades. If partner

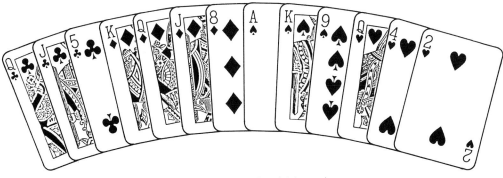

An exploratory opening bid to show shape: one diamond.

BRIDGE

opens One Club, respond One Diamond, but if he opens One Heart, then respond One Spade.

Make the same minimum response whether you have anything between 6 points and 15 points. As an exploratory response has such a wide range of strength, the opener will be forced to bid again in case you have a good hand–you will specify your strength more accurately later. The jargon describing this principle is: 'a change of suit response is forcing'.

Your partner has bid one club. You have enough to respond. You have two four-card suits – diamonds and spades. In these circumstances, show the 'lowest' of the two suits you hold in terms of seniority – remember the ranking of suits, clubs, diamonds, hearts, spades – and bid one diamond.

In selecting a response with less than 10 points, you should show a suit at the One level in preference to responding One No-trump. For example, suppose you have 7 points and your only four card suit is hearts. If partner opens One Club or One Diamond, respond One Heart; but if he opens One Spade you should respond One No-trump.

Limit bids

A limit bid defines the strength of your hand to within one trick. The bid tells partner in which of the ranges 6–9, 10–12, 13–15, 16–18 etc. your hand falls. All limit bids are 'non-forcing', i.e. partner knows your strength and therefore is not compelled to bid again. So it is essential, when making a limit bid, to bid the full value of your hand. Compare these three auctions and see what you think the strength of West's rebid is:

	West	East
	West	*East*
A.	1♥	1♠
	2♥	
B.	1♥	1♠
	2♠	
C.	1♥	1NT
	2NT	

Before we work out West's strength let us say something about his shape. In Example A, West must have less than four spades (or he would have raised East's spades) and at least five hearts (each time you repeat a suit which partner did not support, you logically promise at least one extra card in the suit). In Example B, West should have four spades; in Example C he is reasonably balanced in shape.

Now, what about strength? In Example A, did you think West needed 16–18 points to raise the level? Wrong! East's

change of suit was forcing, West had to rebid. If he had long hearts his only sensible rebid was in hearts and Two Hearts was the minimum he could rebid. So West has 13–15. If he had, say six hearts and 16–18 points he must rebid Three Hearts to show the extra trick.

Example B is similar. If West has four spades he must support East; he has done the minimum possible and therefore has 13–15 points; With 16–18 he should have raised to Three Spades.

Example C is totally different. East's response of One No-trump was a limit bid of 6–9 points. If West had any balanced hand in which there was no prospect of game he would pass. His actual raise to Two No-trumps therefore shows something like 17 or 18 points. If East has 8 or 9 points he should accept the invitation to game by going on to Three No-trumps.

(Next page) The British team receive their medals for winning the 1991 European Championships in Killarney. Standing, from left to right: Ernesto d'Orsi of Brazil (President of the World Bridge Federation) Graham Kirby, Tony Forrester, Andy Robson, Jose Damiani (President of the European Bridge League) Tony Sowter. Front row from the left: David Burn (Coach), John Armstrong, Sandra Landy (non-playing captain) and Roman Smolski.

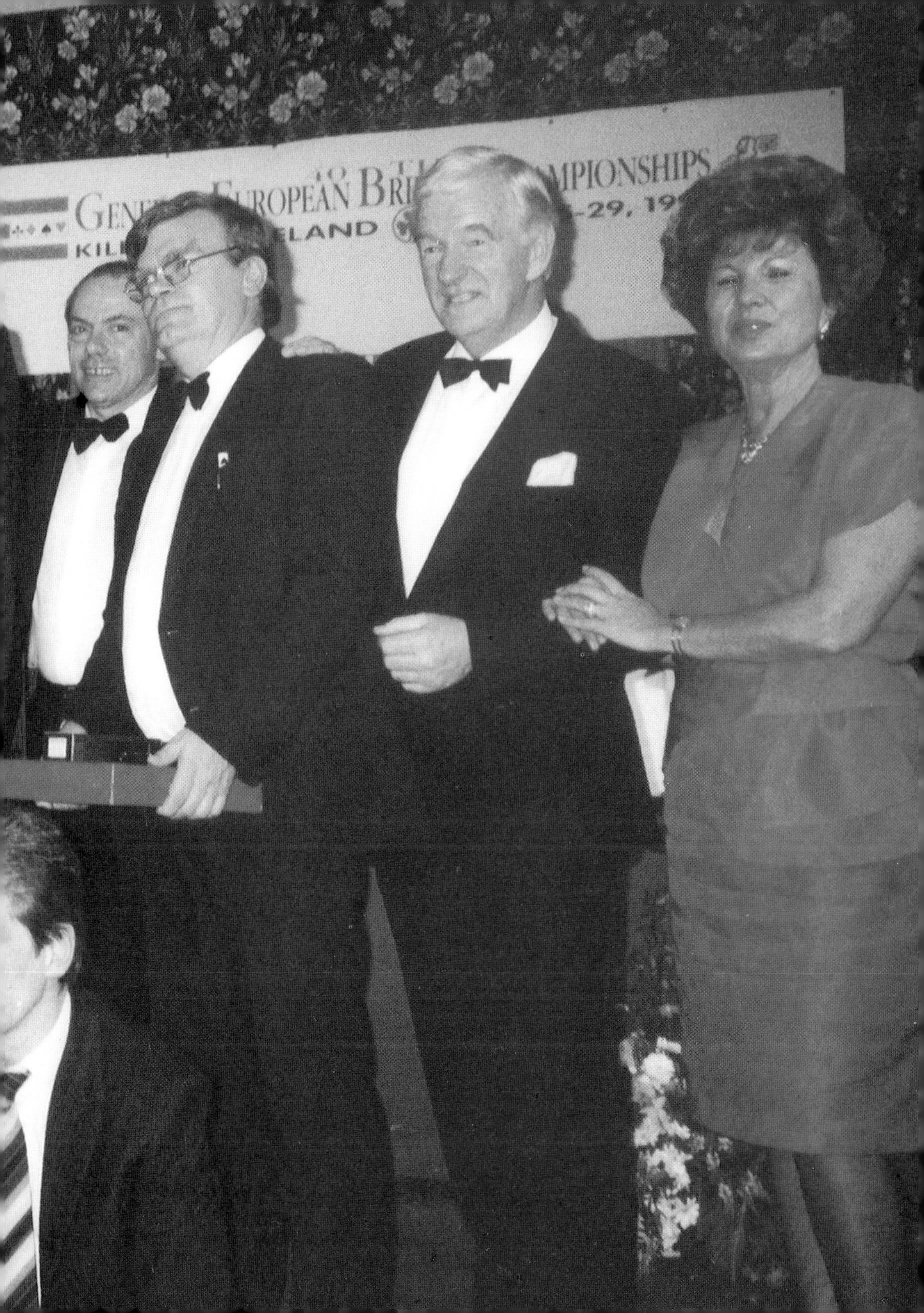
EUROPEAN BRI
MPIONSHIPS
ELAND

BRIDGE

The most common conventional bids

The most important convention of all, and one which all bridge-players use, is called 'The take-out double'. Unluckily for beginners it is the most difficult to understand so we will return to it in a moment. The others in popular use are:

A typical hand for an opening of Two Clubs in the ACOL system.

The Opening Acol 'Two Clubs'. In the ACOL system this shows a very strong hand (at least 23 points) but promises nothing about shape–the bidder could even be void of clubs! The purpose is to ensure that partner keeps bidding even with a weak hand. Clearly, *he must not pass* Two Clubs.

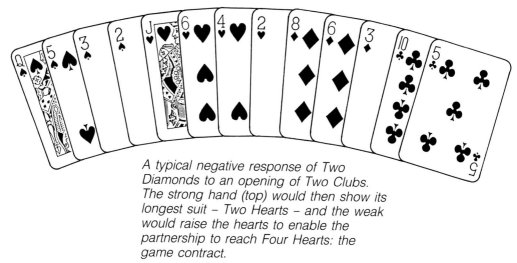

A typical negative response of Two Diamonds to an opening of Two Clubs. The strong hand (top) would then show its longest suit – Two Hearts – and the weak would raise the hearts to enable the partnership to reach Four Hearts: the game contract.

The negative response to an opening Two bid Usually responder makes the same bid (one level higher, of course), as he would have done after a One level opening. However, following the strong opening, responder needs to have a response which says 'I would not have responded if you had opened at the One level'. In the ACOL system, the negative response to Two Clubs is Two Diamonds, and to other Two bids is Two No-trumps. These responses are conventions. Thereafter the partners bid naturally.

The Blackwood Four No-trumps This is a bid requesting partner to show how many aces he has. Amazing that you can devise such an idea! It is used when contemplating a slam call. Partner responds Five Clubs with no aces, Five Diamonds with one, etc. The player who used Blackwood can now deduce how many aces the opponents have, and therefore avoid bidding a slam missing two aces. Ingenious stuff!

The Stayman Two Club response to One No-trump This is used to explore for a major suit fit but we say no more than that because it is outside the scope of this book. We mention it merely because it is used by many average players. If a strange partner says 'Do you play Stayman?', for the moment say 'No'.

If partner opens One Heart, you can use the Blackwood Four Notrumps convention, if you held this kind of hand, to find out if your partnership is missing two aces.

Your partner bids One Heart and your right-hand opponent overcalls One Spade. Bid Two Spades to find out if your partner has long hearts or a balanced hand. Bidding the same suit as your opponent forces another bid from your partner.

The bid of a suit already proposed as trumps by an opponent It is so unlikely that one would wish to have the opponent's suit as trumps that such a call is used to force another bid from partner. Bidding their suit usually is saying to our partner 'I have a game-going hand and wish to explore'.

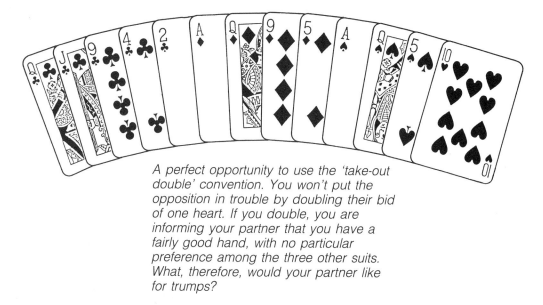

A perfect opportunity to use the 'take-out double' convention. You won't put the opposition in trouble by doubling their bid of one heart. If you double, you are informing your partner that you have a fairly good hand, with no particular preference among the three other suits. What, therefore, would your partner like for trumps?

The take-out double This is the most used of all conventions. Suppose an opponent has opened the bidding at the One level with a suit–any suit, clubs, diamonds, hearts or spades. From the earliest days of bridge, players discovered that they were extremely unlikely to have the hand to ensure that the opponent's One level opening would fail. They therefore never used the call 'Double' which normally means you expect your opponents contract to fail. However, very often, they had a hand on which they wanted to bid but with no strong preference between the three suits excluding the one named by the opponent. Some unknown genius came up with this idea: 'If I double an opening bid at the one level I will not mean I expect it to fail. Instead, I will mean that I have the strength to justify entering the auction but wish you, partner, to select the trump suit'. This agreement solved so many problems that it has become universally popular. The player who makes the take-out double should have at least the strength to open the bidding and 3 or 4 cards in each of the three suits other than the one named by the opponent. Partner must respect the agreement and select a trump suit even with a very weak hand, if the alternative is to allow the opponent to play in a doubled contract he is sure to make.

John Armstrong was a member of the British Open team which won the gold medal in the 1991 European Championships held in Killarney. He was also a member of the British Team which won the silver medal in the 1987 World Championships held in Ocho Rios, Jamaica.

TECHNIQUES · OF · PLAY

When, as declarer, you first see dummy, it can be a daunting moment. The secret of success is to have a plan, and the foundation of forming a plan is to 'count your tricks'. Suppose your contract is Three No-trumps, West leads a spade, and this is what you see:

You are declarer, and the contract is Three No-trumps. You need to make nine tricks. Where are they going to come from?

Dummy

♠ A Q 5
♥ K 6 3
♦ K J 7 6
♣ 6 3 2

```
        N
    W       E
        S
```

Lead: ♠ 2

Declarer

♠ K J 7
♥ A 4
♦ Q 10 5 3
♣ K 7 5 4

You are South. You opened One No-trump and North raised to Three No-trumps. You have to make nine tricks. Look at each suit in turn. In spades you have between the two hands four top cards (A,K,Q,J) but you will only be able to make three tricks because after three spade tricks have been played, you would have no cards left in either hand. In the heart suit you have two tricks (ace and king). In diamonds you have four high cards (K,Q,J,10) but an opponent has the ace. You will be able to make three of the four tricks but to do so will have to lose the lead. So, we count three spade tricks, two heart tricks and three diamond tricks. To make our contract of nine we need one more from the club suit. Can you see a chance for this? To lead a club from the South hand will achieve nothing. Either an opponent will win cheaply or, if you played the king, beat it with the ace. But if you lead a club from the North hand, East has to play *before* you decide whether to play your king. If East held the ace, he would be unable to prevent your king making a trick–whether he won the ace at once, (allowing your king to take a later trick), or whether he played low (allowing you to win with the king at once). What, you will be asking, if West has the ace? West plays AFTER South and will only play his ace after you have played the king. You may find this puzzling but the truth is that you should assume East has the ace because, if West has it, your king is dead anyway. Half a chance of a trick is better than none. This technique, called the **finesse,** is the most important one in bridge, so we will give another example: Imagine this is your holding in a suit, any suit, say clubs.

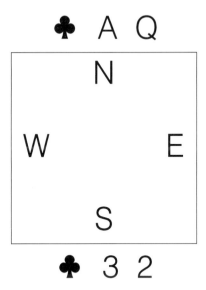

The most important playing technique in bridge: the finesse. Play from the South hand, hoping that West has the king of clubs. If West plays low, then play the queen from dummy.

The ace will make one trick, but what chance is there to make two? There is no hope if you lead from the North hand but if you lead from the South hand and *assume* West has the king you hope to make two. If West plays the king (unlikely) you beat with the ace and then make the queen. If West plays low you *must* try the queen. The queen will win if West held the king. If East has the king the finesse will lose ... but it was worth a try, because it was your only realistic chance to make two tricks.

Now return to the original full hand we gave you. You have a plan to make nine tricks: three spades, two hearts, three diamonds and one club if East has the ace. Which suit should you lead at trick two? A novice is inclined to take his immediate winners but that would lead to disaster here. Having made the spade and heart winners you would have to lead a diamond. The opponent who gained the lead would have winning hearts and spades to play. Instead you must 'knock out' the ace of diamonds while you still have winners in spades and hearts to gain the lead back again. The tip is 'establish tricks early, cash them later'. So at trick two, play the *diamonds* until the ace is gone. Win the spade or heart return and continue diamonds. When the lead is in dummy, lead a club. If East plays low, say a little prayer and try the king. If it wins you can see your way to nine tricks and so now 'cash' all your winners.

Trump play

When your contract is trumps there are two extra matters to consider. Here is an example:

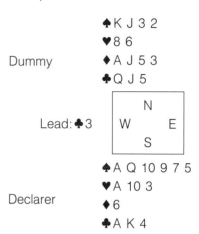

Dummy
♠ K J 3 2
♥ 8 6
♦ A J 5 3
♣ Q J 5

Lead: ♣3

```
    N
W       E
    S
```

Declarer
♠ A Q 10 9 7 5
♥ A 10 3
♦ 6
♣ A K 4

You, South, opened One Spade, North raised to Four Spades, and you, with plenty to spare above a minimum opening, courageously tried for the slam bonus by bidding Six Spades. Can you make twelve tricks? (West leads a club.) In top tricks you count six in spades, one in hearts, one in diamonds and three in clubs, making eleven. Where is the twelfth?

By **ruffing,** – that is, by leading a side suit from the hand opposite a void and trumping in the hand with the void–you can make your twelve tricks. In this way you make your trumps separately because you are not following suit. Your first idea might be to lead a diamond to the ace, creating a diamond void in the South hand; and then lead a low diamond from the North hand, trumping in the South hand. You have won a trick, it is true, but you have not created an *extra* trick, because you have no more than the six trump tricks we already counted. To create an extra trick you must lead a side-suit from the hand with the long trumps (i.e. South) and be able to trump in the short trump hand (North). Then you will have made a trump and still make the six trump tricks you originally counted, i.e. seven in all. The only side-suit which can be trumped in dummy is the third heart. So this is your plan: win the club lead, and *draw the opponents' trumps*. This means playing trumps until they have none left. You do not want them to be able to trump one of your side-suit winners. You have ten trumps, so they only have three. Play out trumps until these three have gone. You must not go on playing trumps or you will have no trump left in dummy to take care of your third heart. So, when their trumps are drawn, switch to hearts, even though this means allowing them to win a trick (you have the ace to take care of one round but they must win the next.) You can win any return by them, and when the lead is in the South hand, lead your third heart. This is a loser, but the North hand is now void so you can play a trump and win the trick. All the rest are yours, the slam is made!

This example illustrates the three key phases of trump play: drawing their trumps, ruffing your own losers, and retaining some trumps to regain the lead

after you have lost it.

There are many more techniques of play, enough to spend a lifetime learning them. That is part of the fascination of bridge–there is always something new to discover.

The opening lead

If there is one moment when the experts make the wrong choice more often than any other, it is on the opening lead. You have only the sight of one hand and the auction to guide your choice. Once the lead is made you can see dummy as well, an enormous benefit. The best we can do to help is to give a few simple tips.

Against no-trumps lead your longest suit. You hope declarer will run out of cards in the suit, so your long cards are winners when you gain the lead later on.

Against a trump contract, if you have a singleton in a side-suit, lead it. You hope partner will win and return the suit for you to ruff.

It is better to lead from a suit headed by a sequence of high cards than one in which the high cards are not in sequence. For example, if the contract is Four Spades and you hold ...

♠ 8 4　♥ A J 3 2　♦ 9 7 3　♣ K Q J 2

It is your opening lead, and you are defending against a contract of four spades. Which card? Look to the high card at the head of a sequence – the king of clubs.

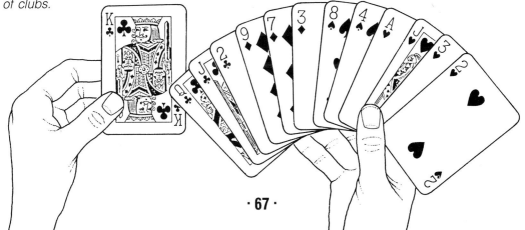

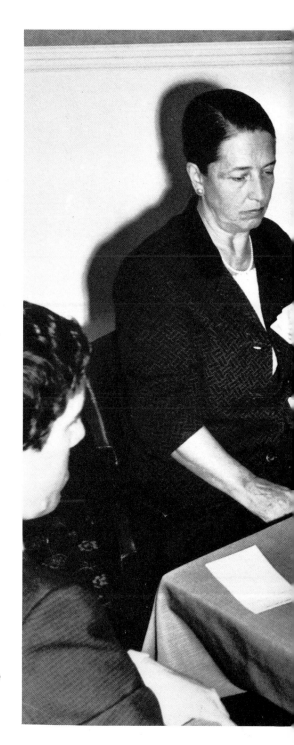

Bridge in the 1950s. The late Jeremy
Flint, on the right, gave up a career in
Law to become one of the first full-
time bridge professionals in Britain. He
subsequently became well known to
the public as the presenter of several
television series on bridge.

It is much better to lead a high club than the ace of hearts. There are two sound reasons for this. First, if you lead the ace of hearts you will capture no big card of the other side, whereas if you wait you may have the chance to make the ace *and* jack. Secondly, if you lead a club it will not be disappointing if declarer wins with the ace. He was always going to make his ace sometime, and meanwhile you have set up a club trick or two which you hope to make when you gain the lead with the ace of hearts. When you lead from a suit headed by a sequence it helps partner if you lead the *top* card in the sequence–here, the king. (If you lead the queen of clubs partner might put on the ace, not realizing that you had the king.)

When you lead from a suit not headed by a sequence, e.g. from K 8 4 3 2 against no-trumps, lead a low card, retaining the king for later. Once again, it helps partner to know what you hold, if you lead a specific card. In Britain most players agree to lead the *fourth* highest of their longest suit. From K 8 4 3 2 this would be the three. How can this help partner? Imagine you are the defender who is not on lead. The opening lead against Three No-trumps is the two of spades. What conclusion can you draw? If the man on lead has led fourth highest of his longest suit and you can also see it is his lowest card, *then he must have precisely four cards in the suit!* You can see how many there are in dummy and your own hand, and therefore deduce how many declarer has.

What constitutes a sequence of high cards? From three high cards in a row always lead high. e.g. from Q J 10 2 lead the *queen*. Do the same if there are two in a row, with the third just one card out from making a sequence, e.g. from Q J 9 2 lead the *queen*. When you have only two cards in a row, e.g. Q J 3 2 we suggest you lead low against no-trumps, but high against a trump contract, where

the first two rounds of a side-suit are what matters (declarer often trumps the third round).

We have already explained why leading an unsupported ace can be bad. However, should you decide to lead from such a suit, lead low against no-trumps, but lead the ace against a trump contract (if you lead low, declarer might win with the king, and when you play your ace later, trump it!).

Signalling

The Laws permit partners to have prior agreement about the meaning of their bids. Similarly, we have 'agreed' opening leads (top of a sequence, fourth highest from suits not headed by a sequence, etc). There is another important area in which a defender can assist his partner by the choice of card played. When discarding, or when following suit but not attempting to win a trick, a defender often has a choice of card to play. Provided this does not spoil his chance of winning a trick later on, the defender can use his choice to guide his partner.

For example, a common agreement is this: 'If I discard an unnecessarily high card when known to have a smaller one, I am indicating a desire for you, partner, to lead that particular suit when you next have the chance'.

Declarer wins your partner's lead, and draws trumps. What would you discard from these holdings in a side-suit; say hearts?

(a) ♥ 10 8 4 3 2

(b) ♥ K Q 9 8 3

(c) ♥ K Q J 10 2

(a) The 2. You wish to discourage partner from playing the suit.

(b) The 9. Partner should guess you have a smaller card to

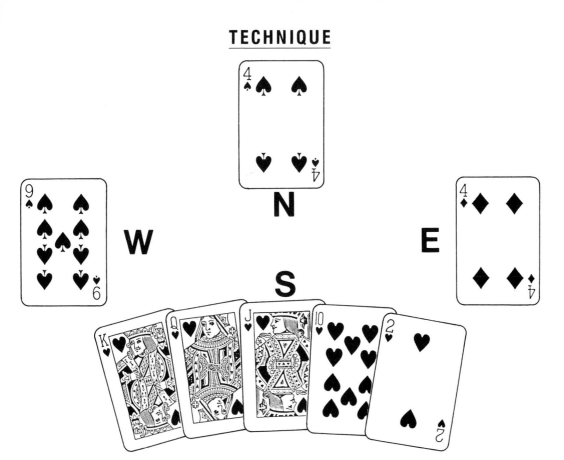

*Spades are trumps; you don't have any,
so must discard from a side suit (hearts).
Discard the king! It's the best way to let
your partner know that you would like him
to lead that suit.*

throw and therefore realize that you would like him to lead the suit.

(c) The King! As it is a trump contract you cannot expect to take more than a couple of tricks in the side-suit. If you discard the 2, your partner will think you do not want the suit led. As you can afford a high one, the clearest message is to throw the highest in the sequence.

This agreement is called 'Signalling your attitude'. It also applies when partner leads a suit and you are not trying to win the trick. Basically, discarding the highest you can afford shows your partner that you like that suit!

Later plays by the defence

There are two tips from whist which are of some help at bridge. These are 'third hand high', and 'second hand low'.

'Third hand high': if your partner has led a low card, and dummy plays a low card, then you should play high even when you expect declarer has the card to

beat you. Quite simply, if third hand also plays low, declarer will win cheaply and still have his high card to beat yours later; e.g. against no-trumps, partner leads the two. Dummy has three small cards and you, third to play, hold J 7 6. You must play the jack even though you expect it to be beaten. To play the six merely allows declarer to win with the eight.

'Second hand low': if declarer leads a low card to a trick, there is usually no need to play high in second seat because your partner who plays last will be well placed to win the trick as cheaply as possible. For example: declarer leads the 2, you are next to play with Q 6 5, in dummy you can see K 8 4. It would be wrong to play the queen 'to force out the king'. Declarer will probably play the king anyway, (or your partner has a cheap trick). Playing the queen in second seat merely ensures it does not win a trick later. However, there are many exceptions to this rule (e.g.you wish to make the only winner for your side before declarer has the chance to start trumping in) so don't rely on it too strongly.

Points of Etiquette

Say 'Hello' to new players arriving at your table.

Introduce yourself to a strange partner.

Keep discussion about your system to a minimum, explaining that you are a novice, have been learning the ACOL system, and use the weak notrump. Mention any of the six conventions you

(Previous page) The British Junior team receive the trophy for the 1989 World Junior title. From the left: Sandra Landy (coach), John Pottage, Gerald Tredinnick, Andy Robson, Raymond Brock (non-playing captain), Derek Patterson, Stuart Tredinnick (twin brother of Gerald) and John Hobson.

feel able to use.

Don't look at your cards until all are dealt. Check you have 13. Hold them up so no-one else can see them.

Avoid mannerisms which might give others a clue to your hand. Take no advantage from any revealing mannerism of your partner. It is best to avoid looking at partner's face during play.

Be careful only to call when it is your turn. Try to work out from partner's calls what is the right contract for the partnership together.

Try to adjust your speed of bidding or play to conform roughly with the norm of those with whom you play. It spoils the pleasure of others if you are much slower, or, for that matter, much faster, than them.

If you become declarer, thank partner for dummy when you see it, even if it is a big surprise. Pause for thought before playing to the first trick. (You should be forming a plan to make your contract!)

If you become dummy *after* your right-hand opponent has led, face your cards tidily in columns with trumps on the right. Do not play any card (not even when following suit with a singleton) unless requested to do so by declarer. If declarer makes the contract, you can say 'well done', but not too effusively. If declarer fails, you can say 'Bad luck', but not sarcastically. It is part of the joy of bridge that good results are ascribed to skill and poor results to bad luck!

If you are a defender be particularly careful only to play a card when it is your turn, and to follow suit.

When play ends ensure both sides agree on the number of tricks taken by declarer.

Do not criticise your partner. Do not gloat over the opponents' disasters. You can apologise to partner at the end of play for any error you made. Be warned, many bridge-players do not follow these rules. Resolve to do better than them in this respect!

The Post-Mortem

Analyzing deals after they have been played is educational and part of the fascination for many. Use the post-mortem to improve your own game, not as a means of laying the blame for some mishap on your partner. Bridge-players who criticize their partners give the game a bad name. Please do not spoil your partner's enjoyment of the game, but don't be afraid to discuss a hand immediately it is over.

If beginners wish to discuss a deal, the best method is to follow a procedure which is always used in duplicate bridge. Instead of the players throwing their cards in the middle of the table they keep them by them so their 'hand' can be re-constituted after play is finished. In duplicate, each of the four hands then goes into a separate compartment of a small tray, and the deal can be given to another table.

When using this method of retaining your cards, there is a simple way to keep track of tricks won or lost. Place the card face downwards pointing in the direction of the side that won the trick. Half way through play the cards on the table in front of you will look something like this, starting at the left:

You have won four tricks (the 1st, 3rd, 6th and 7th) and lost three. Note that you also have maintained the sequence in which your cards were played, so in the post-mortem you could remind yourself of how each trick was played.

In Bridge, there are very few generalizations which hold true on all occasions. So your brain has to go to work checking the logic on each occasion. The mental exercise will do you good. The satisfaction when you solve the problem is immense. Every new deal is a new challenge. You have years of fun ahead.
Good luck!

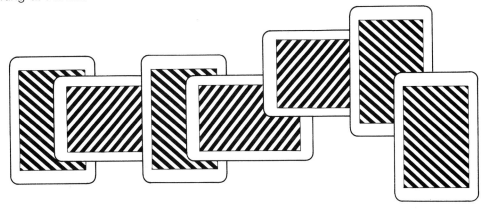

USEFUL ADDRESSES

The British Bridge League
Mrs. A. Gudge,
Secretary,
The British Bridge League,
13 Chaucer Road, Sudbury,
Suffolk.
CO10 6LN

The English Bridge Union
Mr. J. Williams,
Secretary,
The English Bridge Union,
Broadfields,
Bicester Road,
Aylesbury,
Bucks.
HP19 3BG

The Scottish Bridge Union
Mr. T. Workman,
Secretary,
32 Whitehaugh Drive,
Paisley
PA1 3PG

The Welsh Bridge Union
Mrs. M. Aherne,
Secretary,
19 Penygraig,
Rhiwbina,
Cardiff.
CF4 6ST.

The Northern Ireland Bridge Union
Mr. W. Kelso,
Secretary,
9 Upper Malone Road,
Belfast.
BT9 6TD

The English Bridge Union has an office
(Telephone:0296–394414) which sells all
types of bridge equipment, including
copies of the Laws.

The American Contract Bridge League
2990 Airways Boulevard,
Memphis, Tn.
381163847

Your Union will put you in touch with a local bridge club.

**Over one thousand players compete in
the English Bridge Union's annual
Summer Meeting held in the Brighton
Conference Centre.**

RULES CLINIC

INDEX

Page references in **bold** refer to photographs.

auction
  all players to have
    chance to bid 48
  when all players
    pass 48

bids
  illegal 48, 49
  unethical 52

calling out of turn 48
cards inadvertently
    exposed 50
cheating 50

doubling into game 49
doubling partner's bid not
    allowed 49
doubling into slam not
    allowed 49

failing to follow suit when
    able to 50, 51

hands, throwing in 48
hesitation, inferences
    from 52

leading by wrong
    defender 50
leading face
    downwards 50

mannerisms, conveying
    information by 50–2

penalties
  for calling out of turn 48
  for exposing card 50
  for making lower bid than
    previous one 49

for mannerisms 52
for revoke 50
for wrong defender
    leading 50

out of turn, calling 48

redoubling, when & who
    can 49
revoke 50, 51

signalling, secret 50–2

wrong defender
    leading 50
wrong hand, declarer
    leading from 50

INDEX

Page references in **bold** refer to photographs.

ACOL   33, 44, 60
   Two Clubs Opening   60
American Contract Bridge
      League   9
Armstrong, John   **58–9, 63**
auction   12, 26–36, 48,
   see also bidding
auction bridge   8
Austria   9

Bermuda Bowl   9
bidding   12, 20, 22, 26–36
   exploratory   34–5, 54–7
   forcing   13
   illegal   48, 49
   limit   35–6, 42, 54
   no bid   13, 26, 27, 34,
      48
   opportunity to   48
   re-bid   14
   systems   33
   no-trumps   42–4
   three level   44
   two level   44
Blackwood Four No-
      Trumps   61
'Blue Book'   8
bonuses   41
Brighton   **77**
British Bridge League   9

Brock, Raymond   **72**
Buller, Col Walter   9
Burn, David   **58–9**

calling   12
   out of turn   48
   overcall   13, 45
cards   11
   accidentally exposing   50
   seniority of   17
   sorting   19–20
contract   12, 24, 26–36
Contract Bridge,
      development of   8
conventions   12, 54, 60–2
Culbertson, Ely   8, 9
cut   12

Davies, Pat   **7**
deal   13, 18, 26
   redeal   14
declaring   13, 24–5, 26,
      64–7
defender   13, 25
   leading   50, 67–70
denomination   13, 24–5,
      26
discard   13, 21, 70
doubleton   13, 28

doubling   13, 26, 27,
      41–2, 49
   take-out double   60, 62
dummy   8, 13, 24–5
duplicate bridge   9, 10, 75

entry   13
etiquette   74
exploratory bids   34–5,
      54–7
   response   56–7

finesse   13, 65–6
Fischer, Doris   **53**
Flint, Jeremy   **68**
Forbes, Malcolm   **45**
Forrester, Tony   **58–9**

game, definition of   13
grand slam   14, 21, 37, 41

hand
   shape of   27–8
   strength of   27–30
Hobson, John   **72**
honour bonuses   41
honour cards   11, 13

International Bridge
      League   9

Kirby, Graham **58–9**

Landy, Sandra **58–9, 72**
laws 8, 13, 21, 33, 48
lead 13
   opening 13, 67–70
level 24, 26
limit bids 35–6, 42, 54, 57

Macleod, Iain 33
Mahmood, Zia **23, 45**
Mari, Christian **40**

no-trumps 13, 42–4
   weak & strong 44

overcall 13, 45
overtrick 13, 37, 38

partners, choice of 17–18, 26
partnership
   agreements 33
partscore 13
pass 14, 26, 48
Patterson, Derek **72**
penalties 14, 39–41, 48, 49, 50, 52
Plafond 8
point count 14, 28–31
   exercise in 30
   high card points 28
   long suits 28, 29, 31
   short suits 28–30
Portland Club 8
post-mortems 75

Pottage, John **72**
pre-empt 14
re-bid 14
redeal 14
redoubling 14, 26, 27, 41–2, 49
revoking 14, 21
Robson, Andy **32, 58–9, 72**
Rohowsky, Roland **15**
rubber 14, 37
Rubber Bridge 9, 37
ruffing 14, 22, 66–7

score-card 10, 37
scoring 37–42
   bonuses 31, 42
   penalties 39–42
   trick values 37–8
second hand low 74
Sharif, Omar **2**
signalling 70–4
singleton 14, 28
slam 14, 39, 41, 61
Smolski, Roman **58–9**
small slam 14, 41
Sowter, Tony **58–9**
Stayman Two Club
   response 61
suit, following 13, 21
   failing to 21, 22
suits
   long 28
   major 13
   minor 13
   seniority of 12, 18

short 28–30
side 14

table 10
take-out double 60, 62
terminology 12–14
third hand high 71–4
Tredinnick, Gerald **72**
Tredinnick, Stuart **72**
tricks 14, 20–1, 26
   odd trick 13
   overtrick 13, 37, 38
   undertrick 14, 39–41
trick values 37
trumps 8, 12, 14, 22
   choice of 27–8
   drawing opponent's 67
   no-trumps 13, 22, 25, 26
   trump play 66–7
two-clubs opening 60
two level opening 44

USSR 9
undertrick 14, 39–41

Vanderbilt, Harold S 8
Venice Cup 9
void 14, 21, 28
vulnerable 14, 39

whist 8, 20–2
World Bridge Federation
   (WBF) 9
World Bridge Olympiad 9
world championships 9